Educating About/for Food Security Through Environmental Education

An Account of Integration Practices in Teacher Education Programs Across Ontario, Canada

A Volume in Critical Constructions:
Studies on Education and Society

Series Editors

Brad J. Porfilio
California State University, Stanislaus
Marc Pruyn
Monash University
Derek R. Ford
DePauw University

Critical Constructions:
Studies on Education and Society

Brad J. Porfilio, Marc Pruyn, and Derek R. Ford, Series Editors

*Educating About/for Food Security Through Environmental Education:
An Account of Integration Practices in Teacher Education Programs Across
Ontario, Canada* (2025)
by Alishia A. Valeri

*The 2017 Hampton Reader:
Selected Essays from a Working-class Think Tank* (2019)
edited by Colin Jenkins

Read Aloud Handbook for Native American Children (2019)
by Lauren Waukau-Villagomez and Samantha J. Villagomez

*Rethinking Social Studies:
Critical Pedagogy in Pursuit of Dangerous Citizenship* (2017)
by E. Wayne Ross

DIY Punk as Education (2016)
by Rebekah Cordova

Charter School Report Card (2016)
by Shawgi Tell

News Media and the Neoliberal Privatization of Education (2016)
edited by Zane C. Wubbena, Derek R. Ford, and Brad J. Porfilio

*Democracy and Decency:
What Does Education Have to Do With It?* (2016)
edited by Paul R. Carr, P. L. Thomas,
Brad Porfilio, and Julie Gorlewski

Elements of Discussion (2016)
by David I. Backer

*Understanding Neoliberal Rule in Higher Education:
Educational Fronts for Local and Global Justice* (2015)
edited by Mark Abendroth and Brad J. Porfilio

Understanding Neoliberal Rule in K–12 Schools (2015)
edited by Mark Abendroth and Brad J. Porfilio

Immigration and Schooling: Redefining the 21st Century America (2015)
edited by Touorizou Hervé Somé and Pierre W. Orelus

The Phenomenon of Obama and the Agenda for Education (2nd Ed.) (2015)
edited by Paul R. Carr and Brad J. Porfilio

Rebel Music: Resistance Through Hip Hop and Punk (2014)
edited by Priya Parmar, Anthony J. Nocella II,
Scott Robertson, and Martha Diaz

Teaching Marx: The Socialist Challenge (2013)
edited by Curry Stephenson Malott, John M. Elmore, and Mike Cole

Challenging Status Quo Retrenchment:
New Directions in Critical Research (2013)
edited by Tricia M. Kress, Curry Stephenson Malott, and Brad J. Porfilio

Courageous Pedagogy: Enacting Critical Science Education (2013)
by Andrew Gilbert

Dangerous Counterstories in the Corporate Academy:
Narrating for Understanding, Solidarity, Resistance, and
Community in the Age of Neoliberalism (2013)
edited by Emily A. Daniels and Brad J. Porfilio

Can Educators Make a Difference?
Experimenting with, and Experiencing, Democracy in Education (2012)
edited by Paul R. Carr, David Zyngier, and Marc Pruyn

Pedagogies of Deveiling: Muslim Girls and the Hijab Discourse (2012)
by Manal Hamzeh

Power, Resistance, and Literacy: Writing for Social Justice (2011)
edited by Julie A. Gorlewski

Critical-Service Learning as a Revolutionary Pedagogy:
An International Project of Student Agency in Action (2011)
edited by Brad J. Porfilio and Heather Hickman

The Phenomenon of Obama and the Agenda for Education:
Can Hope Audaciously Trump Neoliberalism? (2011)
edited by Paul R. Carr and Brad J. Porfilio

Critical Pedagogy in the Twenty-First Century:
A New Generation of Scholars (2011)
edited by Curry Stephenson Malott and Brad J. Porfilio

Parental Choice?:
A Critical Reconsideration of Choice and the Debate about Choice (2010)
by P. L. Thomas

Educating About/for Food Security Through Environmental Education

An Account of Integration Practices in Teacher Education Programs Across Ontario, Canada

By

Alishia A. Valeri

INFORMATION AGE PUBLISHING, INC.
Charlotte, NC • www.infoagepub.com

Library of Congress Cataloging-in-Publication Data

CIP record for this book is available from the Library of Congress
http://www.loc.gov

ISBNs: 979-8-88730-741-1 (Paperback)

   979-8-88730-742-8 (Hardcover)

   979-8-88730-743-5 (ebook)

Copyright © 2025 Information Age Publishing Inc.

All rights reserved. No part of this publication may be reproduced, stored in a retrieval system, or transmitted, in any form or by any means, electronic, mechanical, photocopying, microfilming, recording or otherwise, without written permission from the publisher.

Printed in the United States of America

CONTENTS

Abbreviations .... *v*

1. **Introduction** *1*
   Linkages Between Food Security, Environmental Education, and Teacher Education *4*
   Overview of the Study *5*

2. **Understanding Food Security Through Environmental Education and Teacher Education** *9*
   What Is Food Security? *9*
   The Food Situation *12*
   Causes of Food Insecurity *13*
   Solutions: Change Is Needed *18*
      The Application of Sustainability for Food Security *19*
      Grassroots Initiatives: People Centered Solutions *20*
      Local *22*
      Educational Systems *23*
         Schools and Teachers *24*
      Food Security and Environmental Education *24*
      Food Security, Environmental Education, and Teacher Education *28*
   Approaches to Integration of Environmental Education in Teacher Education Programs *29*
   Challenges to the Integration of Environmental Education in Teacher Education Programs *32*

iii

3. **Theorizing How to Integrate the Topic of Food Security in Teacher Education** 37
   Ecojustice Education 38
      Language and Root Metaphors 40
      Commons, Commons Thinking, and Enclosure 45
      Approaches to Teaching and Learning 48

4. **The Study** 53
   Qualitative Research Design 53
   Data Collection 57
   Data of Interviews and Documents 00

5. **Integration Practices on the Topic of Food Security in Select Teacher Education Programs in Ontario** 69
   Integration at the Program Level 71
   Integration Strategies at the Classroom Level 79
      Community-Based Learning: Connections to School and the Community 79
      Developing a Global/Local Outlook of Food Security 83
      Evolving Toward Cultural Ecological Analysis 83
   Challenges to Integration Practices 85
   Thinking the Way Forward for Future Integration 87

6. **Integration by Way of Perspectives on the Topic of Food Security** 91
   Sustainable Cultures Perspectives on Understanding the Topic of Food Security Through Integration Practices 92
   Western Modern Cultures Perspectives on Understanding the Topic of Food Security Through Integration Practices 101

7. **Conclusion—What to Do About Integration?** 113
   Summary 113
   Implications for Integration 124
   Contributions to the Literature 128
   Limitations and Delimitations of the Study 130
   Future Research 131

References 133

About the Author 161

ABBREVIATIONS

Environmental Education (EE)
Education for Sustainable Development (ESD)
Education for Sustainability (EFS)
Environmental Education for Sustainability (EEFS)

CHAPTER 1

INTRODUCTION

"Why the topic of food security? What made you think of doing this at this level (of education)? Your topic (the topic of my doctoral dissertation) is quite interesting. I'd like to see how this plays out." All questions and comments asked to me during my doctoral studies, after conference presentations, during interviews conducted for my data collection, and in conversation about what I am doing at this point in my life. My response is not singular in reason, and it is based upon multiple influences compounding at once: familial, educational, professional that built up over time and culminated in trying to find answers for why and how food security and insecurity exists, and what is being done to address the issue. I often asked myself why I didn't learn anything about this when I was in school—perhaps I just didn't know where to look as I progressed through my educational journey, or it just wasn't there.

What I did learn through observation, through listening and often through asking a multitude of questions of many family members (my parents, uncles, aunts and grandparents) is a love of food, and the innate creativity that food and its preparation can bring out in an individual. Even more so, I learned and was involved in the role of food cultivation—the harvesting and growing of multitudes of fresh fruits and vegetables. Through these experiences, I gained a tremendous amount of insight into how food cultivation can secure not only direct access to food but its quality as well.

Educating About/for Food Security Through Environmental Education: An Account of Integration Practices in Teacher Education Programs Across Ontario, Canada, pp. 1–7
Copyright © 2025 by Information Age Publishing
www.infoagepub.com
All rights of reproduction in any form reserved.

At the same time, I also learned from my grandmother about the experiences of food insecurity (although it was never called that). While my grandparents were always bound to the land, literally and figuratively, they endured the hardships of the Great Depression and the Second World War. I recall the stories my grandmother told of their survival linked to producing, gathering and hiding of food—as it was a time of great scarcity tied with economic and political sanctions. My grandmother still tells me of her "tricks" of securing food in hidden corners of their house and buried morsels of food packed under planks of wood—it was a means to an end. Their stories illustrate the necessity of food, coupled with a respect for the sanctity of food. To me, these experiences are my teacher, along with the stories of the past—that their lives were filled with experiences of hunger and poverty. These narratives (past and present) of the love of food and, conversely, the lack of it—tied to their survival and their way of getting through pushes me to want to know more.

As my familial experiences coalesced with my educational (social sciences) and professional experiences (teaching) often taking place in urban settings, I became increasingly curious around the *whys* of food security and insecurity, the effects it has upon people in terms of health (in all regards: mental, physical, emotional, social and spiritual), a person's sense of belonging (when you have food and when you don't), and the impacts of food upon the environment (as I only first experienced gardening from a familial perspective in my late 20s).

My short time teaching at the elementary level (before pursuing graduate studies) exposed me to seeing food insecurity amongst youth and the effects it had on youth health, their ability to learn, and to interact with others during class time. My experience in the elementary classroom also showed me the influence that teaching—what we teach, how we teach, and how it is conveyed affects what one can learn.

Fast forward to the present, where I have an immense opportunity to learn and engage with academic literature on the topic of food security and the food system. As I began creating this research project, I would hear and see food-related issues more frequently. These occurrences made me consider what other people are potentially learning, and in what way they are learning about the issue. For me, *how* I was learning about food security and insecurity during the beginning phases of my research project was both a combination of past experiences, academic literature, and daily viewing of the media. The combination helped me to realize that the topic of food security and insecurity is, in fact, presented, conceptualized, and debated differently depending on the context.

I am learning about and witnessing the effects of a pandemic upon the global food system. In effect, this pandemic is highlighting already existing stressors upon the food system (Beaumont, 2020; Harris, 2020a).

Examples of these stressors as they interact with food insecurity are climatic changes, rising food prices, unsustainable agricultural practices (Dinshaw, 2016), and loss of biodiversity (Watts, 2019). Additionally, the pressing problem of the treatment of migrant workers is also exacerbated in terms of workers' safety and labor rights (Grant & Blaze Baum, 2020; Harris, 2020b). Food insecurity levels amongst Inuit peoples of the far north of Canada are on the rise despite government intervention programs geared at reducing hunger (Murray, 2019) and could worsen in the near future (George, 2020). With directly related issues of increases in food waste and the strain of a growing world population set to reach 9.8 billion by 2050, there is continued pressure placed on the world's food supply (Held, 2017; Westfield, 2013).

Furthermore, due to the productivist nature of the dominant form of food production in the global food system,[1] there are increasing inequities shifting the supply of and demand for food (Brown, 2012a). As a result of the inability of the individual to meet basic nutritional needs, problems such as diabetes are on the rise (Bloch, 2014), as well as hindrances to access foodstuffs such as fruit, vegetables, and meats (Evans, 2017; Sagan, 2017). There is also the psychological stress that occurs because of the lack of access to food either as a result of distances from food sources and/or financial problems fuelling a constant worry about how to feed themselves and others (Kukaswadia, 2014).

Canada has a growing food insecurity problem. Research from Proof (a food insecurity research group at the University of Toronto), indicates that within the 10 provinces in 2021, 15.9% of households experienced food insecurity, with this number equating to 5.8 million people considered to be food insecure. Within the 5.8 million people in Canada, 1.4 million are children under the age of 18 (Tarasuk et al., 2022; see also Caron & Plunkett-Latimer, 2022). From a provincial standpoint, Alberta had the highest of rates of food insecurity at around 20.3%, with New Brunswick with the second highest at 19.0% and Saskatchewan having the third highest with 18.8% in 2021. Within the territories: Nunavut has the highest rate of households demonstrating food insecurity with a rate of 46.1% (statistics are from 2019), and with the Northwest Territories at 23.1% and with the Yukon at 15.3% (Tarasuk et al. 2022). Food insecurity in Canada is largely a result of financial difficulties, and according to Statistics Canada (2020), Canadians who didn't earn an income because of the global pandemic of 2020 were (at the time of reporting) "almost three times more likely to be food insecure than those work worked" (p. 4). Financial difficulties cause increases in food bank use. The increase in food bank use positions the use of food banks as a norm, rather than a temporary measure to alleviate food insecurity (Fraser & Pascoal, 2015; Grant, 2012, 2014) with the demand considered to be continuing in an upward direction (Britneff,

2020). Additionally, Canada's food insecurity problem rests in the amount of available farmland. Canadian farms are being sold for development as farmers retire, which in turn increases the loss of land for food production. Farms are becoming bigger but fewer in number and produce much of the crops Canada exports such as corn and soybean, instead of what we can consume for healthy eating, such as vegetable crops. Increasing this type of crop production reduces the biodiversity of crops, lowers soil health, and boosts the use of agrochemicals (Fraser & Pascoal, 2015; Walker, 2014). Moreover, what people eat directly impacts food choice, and food choice in turn affects food production. Food production, in turn, has environmental impacts, and is an issue of sustainability (Lee et al., 2017). Evidently, the chain of events in the food system are linked together and circle back to the state of food security and food insecurity.

Not only are we collectively seeing Canada and the world as having a growing food insecurity problem, but there are also calls to address the situation. Steps needed to address food insecurity in Canada are directed toward the government who has now formed a national food policy, to address income levels to meet the demands of fluctuating food prices, and to recognize the complex, interwoven nature of food and its impacts upon all living entities (Fraser & Chapin, 2017; Government of Canada, 2019; Levkoe & Wilson, 2017). Moreover, schools are seen as places where youth can learn and relearn about food (e.g., how it is grown, the nutritional impacts of various foodstuffs, and the development of cooking skills) (Coppolino, 2016). In essence, the current conditions we are living in and our interactions with food need to change to address the changing conditions in which food is and will exist.

As an educator, this impetus for change resonates with trying to understand what we know about the concept of food security through education, as well as what education can do to advance changes toward states of food security and insecurity. The culmination of knowledge from my familial, professional and academic experiences have narrowed my lens of focus toward understanding how the concept of food security is taken up by others at the intersection of environmental education and teacher education. Keeping in mind my sources of knowledge, I sought out information on the topics of food security, environmental education, and teacher education within academic literature, searching for where and how these aspects coalesced together.

Linkages of the Topics of Food Security, Environmental Education, and Teacher Education

As mentioned above, there is a need to deal with the challenges of food insecurity. One such way is through a new engagement with food—

an engagement that creates new approaches to enhance sustainable food systems (Sage, 2012; Shiva, 2013). Cultivating new approaches to understanding the concept of food security and building and enhancing sustainable food systems starts with building knowledge and awareness of current global, national, and local food practices through education. Educational systems and teachers play a key role in contributing to broadening understandings of food security and insecurity as well as the potential to foster action toward attaining ecological and sustainable, just food systems (Carlsson & Williams, 2008).

Environmental education (EE) is well positioned to develop new forms of engagement with food because of its curricular and pedagogical aims to develop critical thinking, reflection, and action about environmental and sustainability issues (Robottom, 2013). The incorporation of the topic of food security in the field of EE is based on the linkages between food and the environment—that is, how food and the environment intersect and affect each other (Brown, 2012b; Sage, 2012). As such, there is development of research on EE and food-related issues with examples such as Crosley (2013), Breunig (2013) and Harris and Barter (2015), which discuss from varying viewpoints the interconnections between food and the environment. There is also the development of research on the intersection between EE, teacher education and food sustainability demonstrated through the work of Elsden-Clifton and Futter-Puati (2015) in Australia, and Young and Stanley's (2018) work conducted in Canada. My study will contribute to this growing body of literature by focusing on the integration of the topic of food security as an environmental and sustainability—related issue in teacher education programs across select universities in the province of Ontario, Canada.

Overview of the Study

In this study, I sought to explore the integration practices of the topic of food security within select teacher education programs in Ontario, as well as to understand what perspectives are guiding this integration. The purpose of exploring what teacher education programs are doing toward integration of the topic is based on the potentialities of teacher education programs as places where integration can occur. Teacher education programs serve as sites of teaching and learning, whereby the influence of teacher education faculties can reach curriculum and policy development, classroom practices and surrounding communities (Ferreira et al., 2009; McKeown & Hopkins, 2002; Nolet, 2013). Through the documentation and examination of descriptions of integration, there can be implications drawn for future practices that foster sustainable living and allow for a renewed relationship with food as an educative practice.

The conceptualization of this study is through the theory of EcoJustice Education, which builds a way to integrate the topic of food security in teacher education programs. The selection of the theory is premised on the notion that to work toward achieving a food secure world while also maintaining ecological soundness is about creating new ways of thinking about and engaging with food (Shiva, 2005). EcoJustice Education puts forth the notion that we can change our behaviors for collective betterment of all living things through teaching in a particular manner. Teaching needs to be directed toward building the recognition that to be human is to live engaged in a vast and complex system of life, and to understand the well-being of all members of the planet depends on learning how to protect it (Bowers, 2012a; Martusewicz & Edmundson, 2005). Moreover, EcoJustice Educators advance the notion of creating new ways of being and doing in the world. Curricular strategies and pedagogical practices such as community-based learning, cultural ecological analysis and understanding global and local interconnections that focus on developing an understanding that both the ecological and social issues currently facing our world have intertwined cultural roots in modernist thinking (Martusewicz et al., 2011).

Ways of thinking are perpetuated through language used daily, and the language used can reveal taken-for-granted assumptions held by individuals. Taken for granted assumptions are ideas taken to be true, with no need to question or think about them. These assumptions are upheld by perspectives (referred to as root metaphors within EcoJustice) as "the ideological sources from which the culture draws strength and reproduces itself inter-generationally" (Martusewicz et al., 2011, Root Metaphors and Discourses of Modernity Section, 6); see also Bowers, 2001b).

Recognizing the role one's thoughts and behaviors play in creating negative impacts on communities can be shifted to alternate relationships based on just and sustainable communities through education. Thus, the conceptual framing of this study by way of EcoJustice Education provides a foundation upon which I explored the role teacher education plays in advancing new ways of thinking and engaging with food through educational practices.

Through the next six chapters, I will present an account of the integration practices of teacher educators on the topic of food security. As Chapter 1 has shown, I briefly outlined the problem of food security, as well as how I chose to situate the topic within the field of environmental education. Chapter 2 continues with a review of the literature composed of two parts. The first part presents background literature on the topic of food security/food systems, in which I outline definitions of the concept of food security as well as a brief overview of the current global food situation. I then move on to discuss causes and effects of food insecurity and solutions on how to achieve states of food security noted throughout the food security/food systems literature. Part two of the literature review follows with a discussion of environmental education and the linkages and intersections of food security, environmental education, and teacher education. I situated my study within literature on approaches to the integration of environmental education into teacher education.

Chapter 3 presents the theoretical framework of EcoJustice Education used to conceptualize my study. Also, within this chapter, I show connections of the topic of food security to the theoretical framework. In Chapter 4, I explain how I designed my study, and the overall steps I took to collect and analyze the two main data sources: interviews with teacher educators, and document reviews of select Ontario Ministry of Education curriculum and policy documents, and related teaching documents. The choice of the Ontario Ministry documents is twofold: they provide a snapshot of the topic of food security within the documents as well as serve as teacher resources within teacher education programs.

Chapter 5 and 6 present the results of my study, whereby I outline three findings. The first two findings answer my first research question that pertain to what is happening in terms of integration across select teacher education programs in Ontario, and what strategies are being used by teacher educators in these respective teacher education programs. The third finding answers the second research question, which sought to find out what perspectives (root metaphors as reflective of ways of thinking) underpin the integration practices.

In Chapter 7, I discuss the implications of the findings for the integration of the topic of food security in teacher education programs, as informed by EcoJustice Education. Additionally, this chapter closes the book by outlining a summary of my study and the conclusions I drew from examining the data. Moreover, I highlight the contributions my study makes to the literature, the limitations and delimitations of my study, and ideas for future research.

ENDNOTE

1. The productivist nature of food production means that food production is focused on increasing the production of food as a solution to food insecurity through using agricultural methods which produce a lot of food at once, but with noted consequences such as environmental degradation for instance (see Chapter 3 Literature Review Section titled *Causes of Food Insecurity*).

CHAPTER 2

UNDERSTANDING FOOD SECURITY THROUGH ENVIRONMENTAL EDUCATION AND TEACHER EDUCATION

WHAT IS FOOD SECURITY?

There are around 720 to 811 million people globally who faced hunger in 2020, which is an increase of 161 million people from 2019 (Food and Agriculture Organization [FAO] et al., 2021). The concept of food insecurity is said to exist when food is not readily accessible, available, and/or of sufficient quality (Ford, 2009). The degree of food insecurity (i.e., chronic) and the level within a country (e.g., individual, household, or national) vary across contexts and are caused and made worse by a myriad of reasons (e.g., low food supply, climatic instability, and political tensions such as war). Also, food insecurity is associated with issues such as hunger, malnutrition, and poverty (FAO, 2008). In response to food insecurity, there has been action to address the problem (e.g., sustainable agriculture), resulting in efforts to understand the causes of food insecurity and how it is interconnected to other pressing issues, such as climatic instability and economic uncertainties (Brown, 2004, 2012b; Misselhorn et al., 2012).

Educating About/for Food Security Through Environmental Education: An Account of Integration Practices in Teacher Education Programs Across Ontario, Canada, pp. 9–35
Copyright © 2025 by Information Age Publishing
www.infoagepub.com
All rights of reproduction in any form reserved.

Food security as a concept has shifted and evolved over time. There exist around 200 definitions and 450 indicators of food security (Hoddinott, 1999). The multitude of definitions and indicators reflect the changing global conditions at the time in which they were conceptualized. Also, the myriad of definitions and indicators illustrate the attention being paid to food security in not only understanding what the concept could be defined as, but how best to articulate it to create solutions to the problem. Likewise, understandings of food security are shaped in and through various perspectives and academic disciplines, such as nutrition (Hwalla et al., 2016), economics (Rutten, 2013), and agricultural sciences (Beddington et al., 2012). Additionally, how the term is utilized is based on its use as a policy term/tool in government and its application at community, local, household, and/or individual levels (Lang & Barling, 2012; Rehber, 2012; Sage, 2012).

The concept of food security first appeared at the 1974 World Food Conference in Rome, Italy, and was a result of discussions about how to deal with international food problems (Rehber, 2012). Through negotiations which followed from the conference, the concept of food security was defined as "availability at all times of adequate world food supplies of basic foodstuffs to sustain a steady expansion of food consumption and to offset fluctuations in production and prices" (FAO, 2003, p. 27). Conceptualizing food security in this way reflected the issue at the time around the amount, and the supply of food during such events as drought across major grain-producing regions. According to Jarosz (2009) and Sage (2012), these droughts placed a heavy demand on international grain markets, the global food price crisis, rising oil prices and petroleum-based fertilizers.

The next major shift to the definition occurred in the 1980s, whereby the concept of food security emphasized individual and household levels and was defined as the capacity to provide an adequate food supply enough to ensure people acquired food (Pinstrup-Anderson, 2009). Food availability at national, regional, and local levels factored into the conversation. Moreover, food security as an issue required a more holistic approach that moved away from focusing upon the individual in relation to acquiring food toward understanding the connections of food production systems to an individual's or household's ability to access food (Frankenberger & McCaston, 1998, as cited in Rehber, 2012).

The Food and Agriculture Organization (FAO), of the United Nations, and supported by the Committee on World Food Security (CFS) subsequently expanded the definition to include the notion of access to food by vulnerable people.[1] Thus, this new scope of understanding of food security led to the realization that it is not only an issue of supply but also of demand. In 1986, the World Bank produced a report titled *Poverty and Hunger*, which outlined the "temporal dynamics of food insecurity" (Committee on World Food Security, 2012, p. 4). Food security was understood to exist on a scale between *chronic food insecurity* (connected to issues of poverty and lack of income) to *transitory food insecurity* (brought on by natural or man-made disasters) (FAO, 2008). The concept was connected "to three specific goals: adequacy of food supplies, stability in food supplies and markets and security of the access to supplies" (Committee on Food Security, 2012, p. 4).

Indeed, during these periods of changes to the definition of food security, health and nutrition were also a focus, but not simply a matter of people increasing their food consumption, but for people to have nutritional well-being. Thus, by the 1990s, according to Clay (2002, as cited in Rehber, 2012) the concept changed to include the importance of food safety and nutritional balance regarding food composition and micronutrient intake (Berry et al., 2015; Sage, 2012). This focus on nutrition connects to the concepts of hunger and malnutrition with food insecurity since both speak to a lack of taking in micronutrients.[2] In addition, both issues add to the complexity of figuring out how to address food insecurity, because nutritional aspects and intake of food are more than having access to food—but also about the integration of food-related aspects such as quality (Committee on World Food Security, 2012; FAO, 2008).

A revision to the concept took place at the 1996 World Food Summit in Rome, Italy, and formed a definition that stated that food security is achieved "when all people, at all times, have physical and economic access to sufficient, safe and nutritious food to meet their dietary needs and food preferences for an active and healthy life" (FAO, 1996, p. 3). Near the end of the 1990s, the FAO started to produce annual flagship reports that monitored the state of food insecurity in the world, with the first edition published in 1998. By 2001, the state of food insecurity as reported in the *State of Food Insecurity in the World 2001* illustrated the inclusion of a social component to the already existing definition formed in 1996, yet again shifting the concept to be more inclusive of elements that were deemed to affect the state of food security (FAO, 2002).

The definition of food security is generally accepted to contain four dimensions or pillars: availability, access, utilization, and stability. The fourth dimension was added in the latter part of the 2000s. Stability means that the other three concepts are also stable over time. Thus, the last component underscores that the state of food security fluctuates. Overall, the consistency of these elements over time is what determines the level of food security at the global to individual levels (Berry et al., 2015; FAO, 2008).

Another example of a definition of food security is put forth by Rocha (2008) which contains 5As:

- *Availability*: sufficient food for all people at all times;
- *Accessibility:* physical and economic access to food for all at all times;
- *Adequacy*: access to food that is nutritious and safe, and produced in environmentally sustainable ways;
- *Acceptability:* access to culturally acceptable food, which is produced and obtained in ways that do not compromise people's dignity, self-respect or human rights; and
- *Agency*: the policies and processes that enable the achievement of food security.

This definition mirrors similar elements outlined in the FAO's definition presented above. However, as Lang and Barling (2012) state, Rocha's addition of the term *agency* calls for and requires action on the part of policy makers to enact the term.

Food security is a "complex and multifactorial issue" (Godrich et al., 2017, p. 172). Consequently, understanding the variant meanings, elements and dimensions is vital in working toward addressing the problem of food insecurity. Shifts and additions in focal points within definitions will continue as society works toward creating new ways of feeding ourselves (Brown, 2012b; Gardner, 2013; Sage, 2012). Therefore, the inclusion of the concept of agency in Rocha's 5 A approach has expanded the understanding of food security to incorporate an additional element. The incorporation of the additional element helps to illustrate the term as being more than about one aspect (e.g., access) about achieving a state of food security. Therefore, I utilize Rocha's definition of food security to guide my study within this context of everchanging ways of viewing the topic.

THE FOOD SITUATION

This section provides a brief overview of a debate that exists within food security and food systems literature as to why the current food situation exists and how to address it.

Research on food security and food systems indicate the world is facing a food challenge, and as it currently stands, there is a great deal of uncertainty around how to address the problem because of how various elements intersect with each other. As a case in point, the effects of climate change on agriculture are expected to worsen and how these effects unfold will be different around the world (Fedoroff, 2015; Gardner, 2013).

Moreover, as Garnett (2014) states, how the problem of food security is conceptualized directly creates the solutions being utilized to address it. Much research investment has gone into addressing the food security challenge through increasing food production. This focus has led and continues to spark debate whether focusing on increasing food production is in fact the most viable solution to the problem (Ingram, 2011). The belief in increasing food production as a solution was illustrated through the Green Revolution (Godfray et al., 2010). The trajectory toward increasing food production is supported by organizations such as the Food and Agriculture Organization and the World Bank. However, increasing food production is not to occur without taking into consideration how food is produced (FAO, 2016; Gomiero et al., 2011). This fact highlights a prominent concern within the debate, which is how to sustainably feed a growing world population expected to reach 9 billion by 2050. In other words, there is the need to find a balance between feeding billions of people while attending to the environment's natural resources (Delaney & Madigan, 2014).

Many scholars (Fedoroff, 2015; Gardner, 2013; Grote, 2014; Ingram, 2011; Wittman et al., 2011) counter the sentiment that the world will need to increase food production with the notion that there is currently enough food being produced. Rather, the reason for food insecurity is argued to be one of development and distribution. The issue of food insecurity, then, is a social and political issue requiring economic intervention and policy reframing, not a result of long-term production failures.

CAUSES OF FOOD INSECURITY

This section briefly outlines recurring conditions that are said to cause food insecurity—namely environmental, social and political conditions. Moreover, this overview will illustrate that these conditions are intertwined, and have related effects on the state of food security and insecurity worldwide.

The role of environmental conditions in the pursuit of achieving food security can be seen as paradoxical, in that the more food we produce and consume, the more damage is done to the environment. Scholars argue, however, that this paradox is largely the result of how the current global agri-industrial model of food production is premised on continuing the path of food production through high yielding output. The drive for high output is in fact partly fueled by a cyclical situation of environmental degradation (Delaney & Madigan, 2014; Sage, 2013). Agricultural land is cultivated worldwide to produce more food for a growing and increasingly demanding population, yet agricultural producers are decreasing in numbers. For instance, in India, the decrease in agricultural producers is based on several factors, such as not being able to purchase farming products to grow food, and this in turn leads to a loss of income due to being pushed out of the market. Subsequently, agricultural producers are forced to increase how much food they produce (Lawrence et al., 2009; Shiva, 2013). Statistically, recent studies suggest that world food production is projected to increase 60% by 2050 to meet the projected demand that is estimated to develop. Within this scenario, 80% of the projected increase will have to come from higher yields and 10% from increases in the number of cropping seasons per year (Alexandratos & Bruinsma, 2012; FAO, 2016). Yet the production of these amounts may imply significant intensification of production per unit of land in the coming decades, as well as the fact that new land may not necessarily be used to attain these projected amounts of food (Berry et al., 2015). Although the use of modern technologies (e.g., pesticides) may help to physically supply more food, this model and mode of food production is noted to cause soil erosion, the acceleration of the use of natural resources at unsustainable rates, greenhouse gas emissions, and loss of biodiversity (Blay-Palmer, 2010; Brown, 2004, 2012b; Gardner, 2013; Rosegrant et al., 2014; Shiva, 2013).

Competition for land is also a contributor to the problem in the face of increasing urbanization because the conversion and development of croplands for non-farm uses such as biofuel production is taken over by other countries. Land acquisition or land grabs occur when domestic and transnational companies, governments, and individuals take land over either through buying or leasing of land (McMahon, 2013). Land is taken over for several purposes: (a) having countries secure land for food production that is not necessarily available in their own countries; (b) plowing land and clearing forests, or grassland for planting crops; and (c) to integrate land that is being used or has been used for local subsistence into the global food supply chains (McMahon, 2013). These actions could be seen as part of a wider societal mindset reflective of settler colonialist practices which, according to Rotz and Kepkiewicz (2018) is driven by "disparities in class and capital access within settler colonial context" (p. 252). Moreover, land grabbing is increasing rapidly, with several countries leading the way, such as China, India, and Saudi Arabia acquiring land to assist its own country (Fullbrook, 2010; Godfray et al., 2010; McMahon, 2013). For example, a food company based out of the United Arab Emirates would lease 250,000 acres in Sudan for 99 years. The lease is an example of a corporate takeover of land not intended to be used by the people of Sudan. The land is to be used to grow wheat and other grains for the purchase of product going back to the United Arab Emirates and other countries in the Gulf region (Brown, 2012b).

With pressure to produce more food, and the projected socioeconomics of farming, farmers are forced to use modern technologies to keep pace with the demand. Notably, according to Gardner (2013), increased food production could occur through applying more precise and less wasteful irrigation systems, and through the application of fertilization to crop varieties of plants, which have already been altered through breeding techniques. This scenario is reflective of the beginnings of a new Green Revolution to increase foodstuffs globally, or at least the questioning of whether or not a new revolution is required in order to meet the projected amount of food needed to feed the world's increasing population (Fullbrook, 2010; Gomerio et al., 2011; Vogt et al., 2010). Moreover, with the direction of producing more food, the use of genetically modified crops (GMOs) and organisms is viewed as one way to achieve greater food production (Tourangeau, 2017). GMOs are seen as valuable because they are designed to be more resistant to pests and diseases, more adaptable to inclement weather, more nutritious, and are able to produce higher yields which can stay riper for longer periods of time allowing for a longer shelf life and to reach further shipping distances (Gardner, 2013). However, the use of GMOs is not met without contestation. The safety of GM food and crops for human consumption is left as unknown, as research into their use is done to either show: (a) they are as safe for human consumption as conventionally made food and crops, or (b) as a way to continue to conduct research on their safety. In terms of crops, the environmental consequences of herbicide and pesticide use required for growing seeds, and the potential for cross-pollination among crops is cited as a great concern (Canadian Biotechnology Action Network, 2019; Council for Biotechnology Information, 2018; Schurman & Munro, 2010). The use and push for GMOs seeds also contribute to the displacement of farmers from their land, and from participating in farming because of the inability to keep pace with buying the required components for GM seeds, as shown in India for instance (Shiva, 1993; Thaker & Dutta, 2016).

Additionally, as part of the continued impetus to produce more food, there is a significant consequence of food waste. Food waste adds and creates to environmental damage. It is estimated that global food waste releases 3.3 billion tons of greenhouse gas emissions and creates a global water loss of 675 trillion liters per year, as well as increases land change use and soil depletion (Miller, 2012). Food pulled away from human consumption is estimated to be approximately 1.3 billion tons per year of edible parts for human consumption wasted globally (Gustavsson et al., 2011).

Food waste and food loss patterns occur differently across the globe. Within industrialized countries, there are much higher levels of food waste at the consumer end of the food supply chain, whereas in developing countries food waste is characterized by problems with production, distribution and storage (Parfitt et al., 2010). Nonetheless, food waste and loss are continuing to enhance the environmental issues associated with increasing food insecurity while simultaneously affecting the social and economic impacts of food (Gooch et al., 2010; Shafiee-Jood & Cai, 2016).

In line with the consumer end of the food system, the adoption of Western like diets in developing countries from developed countries in terms of higher consumption of meat and dairy products is stated to increase (Garnett, 2013). This drive for increased production of these foodstuffs highlights the environmental impact of food production. Meat and dairy products carry a disproportionately high sustainability burden, particularly in developed countries, and their consumption is increasing rapidly in growing industrialized countries (Berry et al., 2015; Kissenger, 2013). These dietary changes are the result of rising incomes and rapid urbanization in middle-income countries, which directly impact the demand for these foodstuffs (Sage, 2012).

The environmental conditions and the effects of food production are directly related to social and political conditions surrounding the achievement of food security (Delaney & Madigan, 2014). The supply of and demand for food is linked to its availability and pricing, and as these elements continuously fluctuate, so too does our inability to access food.[3] The inability to access food is linked to many factors, such as gender, poverty, social position and/or other limited economic resources. Within high-income countries such as Canada, it is primarily an economic issue (Gardner, 2013; Kukaswadia, 2014; McIntyre et al., 2016). In dealing with the inability to access food within high-income countries, charitable food assistance is often used to alleviate food insecurity. Food banks are part of the charitable food assistance solutions, and their usage is frequently cited as an indicator of levels of food insecurity within a nation. However, food bank statistics only show part of the problem—the statistics show who is going to get food. Consequently, relying on only these numbers to determine levels of food insecurity leaves out the actual number of food insecure households (De Roux-Smith, 2014; Loopstra & Tarasuk, 2015).

Not only is food insecurity directly related to a lack of money, but it is also related to the physical location of food sources (e.g., grocery stores, and farmers' markets) resulting in what are known as food deserts. Food deserts can be defined as neighborhoods or communities with limited access to affordable and/or healthy food services, such as supermarkets. Thus, for all people with a lack of access to food, either through access to a physical location or the means to reach already established food locations, there is the increased chance people will not eat, or will eat what is available (e.g., food with low nutritional status) (Larsen & Gilliland, 2009; Smoyer-Tomic et al., 2006; Vahabi & Damba, 2013). Food deserts also typically exist in low income, highly populated urban areas such as Detroit, in the United States being considered a food desert in and of itself (Dieterle, 2015). Additionally, Canadian cities have pockets of food deserts throughout the country, however less attention has been paid to investigating the issue in rural and remote areas of Canada (Behjat, 2016; see Lebel et al., 2016 for further discussion of rural food deserts). For instance, in Canada's North food insecurity is noted to be the highest in the country, with Nunavut and the Northwest Territories experiencing some form/level of food insecurity at rates such as 57.0% and 21.6% of the population in 2017–2018 (Tarasuk et al., 2022). Overall, Indigenous people experience the highest level of food insecurity in the country, and in particular the Inuit are facing the most extreme circumstances, especially for those living in remote and isolated communities (Council of Canadian Academies, 2014). Along with the cost of food, which is noted to be around two times the amount of foods in central areas of Canada (Nunavut Bureau of Statistics, 2015), this situation is further compounded by a lack of access to traditional foods through less available animals for consumption, and to the fact that transportation passages are not always available to bring store bought food from the southern parts of Canada into stores—both of these elements are a result of climate change (Ford, 2009). Moreover, there is an increased cost of hunting equipment, decreased traditional hunting knowledge, and a lack of time due to market labor activities (whether it is part-time or full-time employment) to hunt or prepare traditional foods for consumption (Ford et al., 2016; Mead et al., 2010; Pal et al., 2013).

Environmental and social conditions evidently are shaping the ways individuals deal with achieving food security or cope with food insecurity. The environmental and social conditions of this problem are *occurring with* political conditions, or as some scholars would suggest, *because of* the political conditions (Schanbacher, 2010). To clarify how the issue of food security is defined or framed, shapes the solutions that are created to address the problem (Tesh, 1988, as cited in Power, 2009). The framing of the problem is based on where the emphasis is placed. For instance, policies and the subsequent practices that follow illustrate where the emphasis is placed, in that if food insecurity is understood to be an issue of low food supply, then practices will lean toward increasing food production. Practices accompanied by research and investments could augment an increase in agricultural technology rather than focusing on research and investments in low-input agriculture, such as organic agriculture and soil fertility management (Garnett, 2014; Rosegrant et al., 2014). Therefore, the perspective taken translates into a policy agenda and demonstrates how governments and/or organizations apply the perspective at various levels within a nation (Lang & Barling, 2012). Consequently, if the focus on policy places too much emphasis toward one side of the food security and/or insecurity issue, other perspectives lose sight. However, there is room for improvement in having policy shape how countries proceed in dealing with food insecurity and unsustainable food systems, such as through reorienting policy changes and policy development. Despite the role that policy plays, countries such as Canada have only recently created a national food policy (Food Secure

Canada, n.d.; Government of Canada, 2019).[4] The lack of a national food policy or strategy maintains a disconnection between departments (i.e., Health Canada, Agriculture and Agri-Food, Service Canada) and results in continuous barriers to physical and economic access to healthy, and culturally acceptable food for all citizens (De Schutter, 2012). Consequently, the significance of having a national food policy creates the space for a coordinated effort across various ministries and jurisdictions (at all levels), that allows for communication to occur across a breadth of food-related issues within parts of a country. Moreover, having a national food policy can illustrate the gaps in need of notice which threaten the achievement of food security, long-term planning, and improved accountability for the goals set out in a national food policy (De Schutter, 2012).[5]

The effects of these conditions outlined above are largely demonstrated through health-related issues of food insecurity. Within the adult population, food insecurity leads to increased instances of chronic ailments, such as obesity, anemia, diabetes, heart disease, and depression. From a psychological standpoint, stress increases for some because of the constant worry about how to feed themselves and others (Kukaswadia, 2014). Moreover, the social impacts that can arise from food insecurity can create stress and conflict with family relationships and friendships. For children, the health effects play out in the form of poorer physical and mental outcomes, inclusive of the creation of long-term chronic health conditions such as asthma and diabetes (Kirkpatrick & Tarasuk, 2008; Thomas et al., 2019).

SOLUTIONS: CHANGE IS NEEDED

As a result of the conditions presented above, there is a growing global response from various sectors of society to advance solutions to the food insecurity problem. This section of the literature review will outline larger concepts within the food systems/food security literature that relate to how the food system could operate, as well as the application of education toward food studies. For the first section, the concepts outlined throughout the literature indicate a direction toward the incorporation of the concept of sustainability, the enhancement of sustainable food practices and grassroots initiatives (food justice and food sovereignty). These concepts are aimed at repositioning a different emphasis on food (from where it currently resides) as part of the food system. All efforts put forth require changes to be made across and within a nation, although how these changes play out need to be context specific. As evidenced throughout the literature review, there is no singular way on how to proceed because not everyone has or will have the same view on how these changes are to take place, or for that matter if the changes are in fact the most appropriate (Garnett, 2014). The second section begins with a review of research in the field of education and food studies focusing on the formal level of schooling as part of a solution to the food insecurity problem. Following this, I transition into a discussion on the intersection of existing research on teacher education, food security, and environmental education.

The Application of Sustainability for Food Security

As demonstrated by the causes of food insecurity throughout the literature examined here, the current path toward achieving global food security is unsustainable. Food security and sustainability need to be seen as aspects that are interrelated rather than separate governance issues to work toward sustainable food security (Lang & Barling, 2012; Sage, 2012; Sonnino et al., 2014). This call is emphasized through a change in the definition of food security, to include sustainability as one of the pillars. That is, sustainability needs to become part of the overall conceptualization of food security (Berry et al., 2015; Hanson, 2013). The adoption of sustainability as a framework puts forward vital principles across biological, economic and social realms—and one of the essential requirements of sustainability is to maximize the achievement across all three realms (Sage, 2012). While this is a goal of sustainability, again there is also the issue of where the concept of sustainability should be applied when it comes to addressing food production, and of how the concept of sustainability itself is to be defined. Godfray et al. (2010) consider this issue by offering possibilities for where sustainable practices should take place, whether it be at the farm, ocean, national and/or global levels, to achieve not only sustainable food security but also sustainable food systems. Although the global level would be the most desirable goal, the application of sustainability to food production is highly site specific and needs to be created by the people who will use and apply these changes (Godfray et al., 2010). A specific example of the application of sustainability in the food system is in agriculture. Sustainable agriculture refers to the notion of a farming system, which imitates natural ecosystems. In effect, sustainable agriculture should have the goals of: preserving the natural resource base with special attention to soil and water, the reliance of minimal use of artificial inputs from outside the farm systems, be able to recover from disturbances caused by cultivation and harvest while at the same time taking into consideration economic and social costs (Pimental et al., 2005). Much like the definition of food security, there are various definitions of sustainable agriculture which vary based on the specific site of its application—in that sustainability depends on the perspective taken when looking at the farming system (Gomiero et al., 2011, p. 14).

In the pursuit of sustainable agriculture to become more commonplace within food production, focusing on only the supply side limits approaches to solving the problem of food insecurity. Food system sustainability or food sustainability is directly related to achieving food security and requires that the whole food system needs to be taken into consideration in creating solutions (Capone et al., 2014; Garnett, 2013, 2014). To reiterate, the production side of the food problem focuses on the need to supply more food, and the demand side of the food problem focuses on the interactions and roles of consumers and food companies. Eating patterns have a significant impact on the environment and on our health. For instance, if consumption of high-impact foods such as animal products is driving supply, companies may respond in kind to meet this demand—companies tailor food products to meet the demand of consumers. Therefore, food systems activities influence not only what is being consumed, how it is produced and acquired, but also who gets access to food, and the quality of the food (Ericksen, 2008).

Grassroots Initiatives: People-Centered Solutions

Part of the perspective of changing the food system focuses on the relationship among actors in the food system. By doing so, emphasis is placed on examining imbalances and inequalities experienced by people. The imbalance is exemplified through dual issues of excess and insufficiency in both the environmental context (over as well as under application of agricultural inputs) and in health and nutrition (e.g., obesity and hunger) (Patel, 2008). The focus is on how the food system is governed, and in effect circles back not only to food production and consumption but also to people's rights to these aspects.

Gaining continuous traction in food system discussions, as part of the overall transformation of the food system, is the idea that people have the right to healthy food and have the right to grow their own food. Both the ideas of food justice and food sovereignty seek to place these changes at the forefront of the food system, because these ideas seek to ensure social justice, ecological soundness, fairness and equity within the food system (Hume, 2010; Shiva, 2005; Wittman et al., 2011). The force with which these ideas are being put forward in food systems literature illustrates the same contention as with the idea of achieving food security. The idea of addressing the overfed and underfed dynamic in the food system is dealt with by understanding the causes of the overfed and unfed problem. Therefore, proponents of these ideas are calling for a reframing of the problem.

Food justice emerged predominantly in northern countries from the environmental justice movement to bring to light the connection between marginalized people and diet-related diseases, underscoring that access to food for certain populations is unfair and unevenly distributed across areas in which people live in both rural and urban areas (Gottlieb & Joshi, 2010; Holt-Giménez, 2011). For communities to be thriving, food justice advocates the idea of the right to food, increases in food safety procedures, and for citizens to become involved in community food systems. Such examples are seen through the promotion of local food with community gardens, urban agriculture, community-supported agriculture, as well as joining and/or forming Food Policy Councils. Moreover, as part of achieving food justice, youth are encouraged to get involved in assessing the food system, school and community gardens initiatives, and work toward raising awareness about food justice through various activities in their respective communities (Holt-Giménez, 2011).

Occurring simultaneously and building upon food justice is the idea of food sovereignty. Food sovereignty as a concept was founded in 1996 by the organization La Via Campesina, or alternatively called the International Peasant Movement in Mexico. The organization is composed of various individuals such as peasants, small to medium scale producers, rural women and youth, Indigenous people, farmers, and landless (peoples) (Schanbacher, 2010). First developed in the global south, food sovereignty is now global in its reach (Wittman et al., 2011, for a Canadian account). This idea puts forth the notion of "the right of nations and peoples to control their own food systems, including their own markets, production modes, food cultures and environments" (Wittman et al., 2011, p. 2). The driving force of this definition, and its movement within the food system, consists of activists, farmers, and citizens embedded in a network of civil society organizations (CSO) (Koc et al., 2008). Depending on the level of change to occur within a country, this concept is seen as the most radical toward changing the food system. The radical part of this concept is based on transforming the food system away from the current industrialized system of food production. The transformation is achieved through altering one's relationship with food to one that is based on an integrated, democratized and localized food system, where sustainability is part of the overall goal of a healthy and just food system (Wittman et al., 2011).

Food sovereignty is generally seen in direct opposition to the concept of food security. The opposition exists because of the ways in which the term food security can be adopted by neoliberal and/or "corporate-dominated biotechnological practices" to deal with the food problem, for instance (Blay-Palmer et al. 2014, p. 185; see also Jarosz, 2014; Schanbacher, 2010, for explanations of both terms). There are proponents of this idea that call for a move away from utilizing the concept of food security (as commonly cited) to enacting the concept of food sovereignty as the way forward.

Local

Local food is seen to fall into this category of providing an alternative way of engaging in the food system from the conventional food system. The term local does not have a precise definition, nor are the definitions held in consensus (Campbell & MacRae, 2012). Like other food-related terms, context plays a role in how the term local is understood and implemented (Ackerman-Leist, 2013). There are many considerations about how the term is put into use. Local is often understood in its relation to physical location and space of food production. In other words, the location or foodshed (the geographic area in which the food supply is derived) defines the parameters of the term local (Peters et al., 2008). However, the physical location and spatial aspects of defining the term local is contested. The contestation rests in that what is considered local or national food is socially constructed. Therefore, it is based on a particular place and time function (Born & Purcell, 2006). This contention can lead to questioning whether local refers to the point at which the consumer receives the food, or at the point of consumption (Ackerman-Leist, 2013).

Also, local is associated with common interests among people contributing to the building of community through the "development of links within everyday life" (Allen et al., 2003, p. 64). Connected to the concept of community is the notion of relationships forming part of the local discourse, whereby consumers form new economic relationships or provide support for people in need (Feagan, 2007). Along the lines of expressing commonalities is the sense of place, or place-based associations made to the term local. For instance, the labeling of the origin of foods being used alongside different foodstuffs such as Napa Valley wine, can elicit and invoke the essence of that particular place (Allen et al., 2003; Ackerman-Leist, 2013).

Local food is seen as an alternative to the conventional food system as a source of food that is intended to "counteract ecological, social and economic impacts of the globalized food system" (Ilbery & Maye, 2005, p. 825, as cited in Franklin et al., 2011; see Mount, 2012). Local food becomes resistance to the negative aspects associated with the industrial food system, and acts as a beacon for ecological sustainability, social justice, democracy, food security or increased food security, and better nutrition (Born & Purcell, 2006). However, local food has some opposition—the opposition is in reference to the assumption that local food is inherently good. Born and Purcell (2006) refer to this as the local trap. Local, as noted, is a socially constructed concept, and cannot be considered inherently better, as social injustice, food insecurity, and the marginalization of people's access to food occur within the local food system. The marginalization of people's access to food is based on low-income consumers not necessarily being able to purchase local food (Hinrichs, 2000), thereby shaping local food to be seen as elitist, exclusive and inequitable (Dupuis & Goodman, 2005; Hinrichs, 2003).

At this point, the struggle to have changes in the food system through an application of sustainability at both the theoretical and practical levels, or through grassroots initiatives, will require finding a common ground on the issue. The evidence presented in the causes of food insecurity section illustrates a lack of insight about how to go forward. For genuine consensus to move forward, shifts in values and paradigms are needed (Fullbrook, 2010; Gomiero et al., 2011). For example, shifts in values and paradigms could occur through: (a) recognizing food as security not a commodity (Fullbrook, 2010), (b) structural changes in the application of sustainability of food (Garnett, 2014; Sage, 2012), and (c) viewing food security and sustainability as connected rather than separated issues (Berry et al., 2015). Thus, what is required is a new way of thinking about our engagement with food, and a new way of organizing our lives that will enhance and sustain food systems (Shiva, 2005, 2013).

Educational Systems

Organizing our lives differently includes exploring how education and our educational systems address the food insecurity challenge. Educational systems play a vital role in contributing to building knowledge and awareness about food (Flowers & Swan, 2016; Koch, 2016), and act as a space to cultivate action toward food-related issues of environmental sustainability in the food system (Carlsson & Williams, 2008). By way of this potentiality of schools and teachers to work toward addressing food-related issues, research illustrates a push toward the education of food (or food education). Food education is a broad term, encompassing a range of formats, such as nutrition education and the use of school gardens (Korzun & Webb, 2014). There is evidence that youth are experiencing poorer health than in the past, and part of the situation is related to poorer eating habits, for instance (Korzun & Webb, 2014). The aims of food education are akin to a resurgence of home economics, as well as the hope of changing the eating habits of youth through nutrition-based programs—as nutritional based programs have the potential to do so (Benn, 2014; Falman et al., 2008).

Schools and Teachers

School food and the policies and practices around food (also termed the provisioning of school food) draw attention to the role that food practices play in our daily lives (Earl, 2018; Morgan & Sonnino, 2013; Priyadharshini & Carrington, 2016). Food is a medium for learning about larger social, political and environmental aspects of food. For instance, food can show the implications of these aspects through how food is produced, consumed, and how healthy food is inaccessible to some people (Lupinacci & Happel-Parkins, 2018; Robert & Weaver-Hightower, 2011; Stapleton, 2019; Weaver-Hightower, 2011).

Moreover, research in food education has picked up on the call for understanding food as an issue of sustainability, as a way of teaching about sustainability, and a medium to broaden its lens toward learning about food security and food mileages (Elsden-Clifton & Futter-Puati, 2015; Janhonen et al., 2016). Often used as a teaching tool for these aims are school gardens. School gardens are viewed as an effective tool to teach about food and sustainability, as well as provide a space for youth to learn how to grow food, reconnect to the environment, build relationships with others as part of a collective food experience, and increase the intake of fruits and vegetables (Berezowitz et al., 2015; Sottile et al., 2016).

In conjunction with the focus on the school level as sites of learning about food, there is recognition that what teachers and preservice teachers know about the agri-food system (Trexler et al., 2000), and nutrition (Unusan, 2007), and the role food plays in the daily lives of low-income and marginalized youth (Stapleton & Cole, 2018) matters for student learning, changing eating behavior, and raising awareness and knowledge of food choices and food security. For change to occur, it is imperative that teachers are prepared to teach about food-related issues, whether about food security (Dhawan, 2014), or about food and nutrition (Perikkou et al., 2015). Therefore, it is vital as Elsden-Clifton and Futter-Puati (2015) state to explore the ways in which teacher education is taking on this issue. Examining how teacher education programs are addressing the food-related issue of food security forms the basis of this research and will be reviewed in the following sections.

Food Security and Environmental Education

Within the broad field of educational research, environmental education (EE) is well positioned to develop knowledge, awareness and capacities to engage with, and enact change to environmental and sustainability issues of which food security is related. EE as a discipline began with the intention to "educate the world's citizens about our relationship with Planet Earth" (Palmer, 1998, p. 3). This intention predominantly resulted in a form of education focused on changing and creating new human behaviors to avoid the continuous depletion of natural resources and pollution. Addressing these aspects of environmental problems took on a largely scientific approach (Gough, 2013). However, this enactment of environmental education was seen as too narrow of a focus, leading the field to evolve over the years to examine, approach and understand environmental problems through a broader lens by making the connections that environmental problems have with social, political and economic aspects (Wals & Kieft, 2010).

Subsequently, with education seen as a driving force to solve these environmental problems, environment-related education practices emerged, causing shifts in the language used in the field of environmental education (Robottom, 2013). This shift led in some cases to EE being implemented alongside related education streams such as Education for Sustainable Development (ESD), Education for Sustainability (EFS), Environmental Education for Sustainability (EEFS), and/or depending on the context in which the educational initiatives are taking place, for EE to be re-termed as one of the related education streams, such as Education for Sustainable Development (Robottom, 2013; see Wals & Kieft, 2010, for a discussion of related terms). Each approach has similarities and differences in their origins, in their content, and in their underlying pedagogical strategies. For instance, EE is noted to have origins in conservation approaches, that inform people and students about the environment, whereas ESD has moved toward a focus on educating individuals to think more critically and reflectively about change and how to bring about a change for sustainable living (Gough, 2006; Sauvé, 2002; Tilbury, 2004; Wals & Kieft, 2010). Research in the field is vast and far-reaching attempting to tackle environmental and sustainability issues from a variety of angles, such as pedagogical strategies (e.g., place-based learning), curriculum development, and the reorientation of teacher training toward sustainability (Reis & Scott, 2018; Stevenson et al., 2013).

Environmental education illustrates development toward the incorporation of food- related issues (Swan & Flowers, 2015). There are several examples, each focusing on the interconnection of food and the environment, of which attend to the concepts of food security as well as food-related concepts, each with a varied context of focus. Crosley (2013) situated her work within urban environmental education to not only augment urban EE, but to highlight the importance of the conditions in which someone lives with the concept of food justice. The placing of the concept of food justice in urban environmental education ultimately brings together the sociopolitical elements of urban areas into focus, and about how these elements both affect the quality and access to healthy food and healthy environments. A study by Lloro-Bidart (2017) examined the impact of neoliberalism on the teaching practices of an Aquarium in the state of southern California, United States. The Aquarium is positioned within a neoliberal funding structure, placed within an entertainment market, and has a commitment to ocean conservation. All these aspects according to the author (and demonstrated as such) affect the teaching practices of the Aquarium, as well as shape the solution put forth by the Aquarium. The Aquarium's solution for ocean conservation is framed through the environmentally responsible action of sustainable seafood consumption. However, the author contends that framing an action without critical awareness of the effects of the solution can continue the same types of practices.

Research conducted in Australia by Davila and Dyball (2015) illustrated the educative value in people growing their own food by using the theoretical frameworks of transformative learning and critical consciousness. The authors suggest that when people learn to grow their own food, or localize food production systems, this in turn creates social and environmental supports, and the realization that an alternative food discourse (food sovereignty) is needed to create a more sustainable food system. Meyer's (2013) research described work on food sovereignty being done in Hawaii through land education initiatives. For instance, the Hawaiian peoples cultivated various foodstuffs such as taro, or kalo which require certain growing conditions. The method to cultivate such foodstuffs is through the ahupua'a system of resource management developed by the ancient Hawaiians to live sustainability within an island ecosystem. This system of resource management recognizes the interconnections between multiple elements in the island ecosystem, such as the interconnection between the mountains and the oceans, and the specific purposes that the different sources of water (i.e., ocean, fresh water and rain) play in connecting them together. Another example, Meyer (2013) highlighted is the Kaiao Youth Garden that was created and is maintained by community members living beside unused lands. This garden allows for the perpetuation of the Hawaiian values and knowledges and is "a small link in the larger chain of gardens, [and] communities" (p. 100), as well as food sovereignty and Indigenous education. In alignment with the previous authors' work toward including a critical line of consciousness and transformative practices into the learning about the food system, Rose and Lourival (2019) argue that this shift can occur through the application of a political economy of food systems lens in EE. By moving in this trajectory, not only is there learning and relearning occurring when it comes to understanding the functioning of the food systems but the possibility of the formation of a socially and ecological just food system. The requirement for this shift is the enactment of food citizenship, which is based on engagement and motivation of people to participate, belong, contribute, and govern their own food environments.

Reis and Ferreira's (2015) study in Australia explored the role that gardens (community and school) play in building social resilience among school-age children and young adults. Specifically, the study focused on how gardens can be sources of assistance during emergencies, issues of food insecurity within the community, and address challenges brought on by climate change. The conclusions drawn from the authors demonstrate that gardens are sources of learning about social resilience and food procurement, and that gardens can foster and cultivate social resilience capacities such as learning and adaption, empowerment and participation, inclusiveness and social ties, and self-reliance and self-organization. Similarly, a study by Malberg Dyg and Wistoft (2018) explored the effect of outdoor activities in the Garden for Bellies school garden program have on student wellbeing. The authors conclude most of the students experienced positive emotions regarding their self-perception and interpersonal relationships. Moreover, the students' connections and interconnections to the natural environment increased by learning about how to treat living things with compassion, and to see themselves as part of nature. Additionally, Mayer-Smith et al.'s (2007) study situated in British Columbia, Canada, discussed fostering an ecological consciousness by the physical act of growing food. Through the intended choice of the medium of food upon which to meet the authors' goal, they created an Intergenerational Landed Learning on the Farm for the environment project. This project brought together community elders and elementary school children, as well as their teachers, working in tandem to cultivate food crops on an urban farm. The results of the study indicated that when intergenerational learning experiences are partnered with working with the land, there is indeed a strong potentiality in increasing environmental concern among young people.

Breunig's (2013) study focused on investigating the influences of environmental studies programs in Ontario, Canada upon secondary students "pro-environmental and pro-social choices about food" (p. 155). The results indicated that food was a very common theme that arose in the focus group discussions with the secondary students. Moreover, through conversations with teachers, the author noted that the topic of food was also incorporated through food education as part of the curriculum. Given the results of this study, it is evident that the participation in the environmental studies programs influenced students "evolving relationship with food" (p. 164). Therefore, a suggestion put forth by the author is for educators to seize opportunities to enact a more formal practice of a food specific curriculum, as a part of the environmental studies programs.

Continuing with the focus on the formal side of schooling, Harris and Barter's (2015) study centred on food and nutrition from the perspective of connecting students to their community through local food in Newfoundland and Labrador, Canada. By designing curriculum using critical place-based pedagogies, students were provided with the opportunity to learn about the importance of place in relation to food production, but more largely to community food security through the concept of food sovereignty. By conducting this study, the authors underscore the need to train teachers about how to engage students in food-related issues and emphasize the importance of building educational leadership for Eco-Justice. The focus of the study attempted to address what food education scholars, and Harris and Barter suggest which is the need to train teachers to take on food-related issues.

Food Security, Environmental Education, and Teacher Education

This study will focus on the role of teacher education in selected Ontario universities as a place where the topic of food security as an environmental and sustainability-related issue is integrated or not integrated. Currently, there are two studies that specifically point in this direction of integrating the topic of food security within environmental education research by discussing the related relationship between food and sustainability. Elsden-Clifton and Futter-Puati's (2015) study conducted in Australia illustrates this integration through the implementation of a workshop in a Bachelor of Education program. As food education tends to focus heavily on nutrition, the authors sought to create and deliver a more critical understanding of food education by merging nutrition and sustainability as nexus points of understanding the link between food and nutrition. The link focuses on the concept of food sustainability. Food sustainability or alternatively phrased as sustainable food systems, is conceptually part of achieving a food secure world. Sustainability in relationship to food mirrors the multipronged dynamics of achieving environmental, social, and political dimensions in the food system (Ackerman-Leist, 2013; Blay-Palmer, 2010; Lang & Barling, 2012). The authors' reasoning for the integration of food education into teacher training is based on the same contentions put forth for infusing sustainability and environmental education into teacher education programs.

Similarly, a second study by Young and Stanley (2018) in Canada illustrates the use of a learning garden alternative placement and eco-mentorship program as part of sustainable environmental education practices. The learning garden alternative placement advances learning about food sustainability and ecological literacy in teacher education using community gardens for "meaningful, active, and integrated learning"

(p. 50). This placement provided the space for teacher candidates to learn through planning gardens and other greening related activities. The intention of the placement was to illustrate a direct mode of integrating the concept of food sustainability into classrooms, as preservice teachers could create learning gardens programs in local schools. In essence, the learning garden alternative placement acted as a line between learning the skills of gardening from expert gardeners, to planning and planting school-based gardens. Moreover, teacher candidates had the opportunity to exchange the learned skills with K–12 students through integrated curricular experiences through their teacher education program.

Given the current research that explores the integration of the topic of food, and more specifically the teaching of the concept of food security within teacher education programs, I reviewed studies from the related area of teacher education in environmental education research to position my study.

APPROACHES TO INTEGRATION OF ENVIRONMENTAL EDUCATION IN TEACHER EDUCATION PROGRAMS

Reorienting teacher training toward environmental learning was recognized in the 1970s by UNESCO as a key factor in developing environmental education (UNESCO, 1978, as cited in Gough, n.d.). The impetus to develop teachers' capacities in EE not only allowed teacher training on EE but also provided a space for EE to be infused in teacher education curricula (Tilbury, 1995). The training of teachers is significant as teachers are seen as key agents of change in society, they have the potential to facilitate learning for environmental awareness, advance understandings of, and promote behaviour changes toward sustainability-related issues (Ferreira et al., 2009; McKeown & Hopkins, 2002; Pedretti & Nazir, 2014; Pedretti et al., 2012). Teacher education faculties and institutions serve as sites with far-reaching influence upon curriculum and policy development, classroom practices, and the surrounding communities toward educating about sustainability and environmental responsibility (McKeown & Hopkins, 2002; Nolet, 2013; O'Gorman & Davis, 2013; Swayze et al., 2012). Moreover, teacher education faculty members directly add to the creation of and distribution of new knowledge through research and publication activities (Di Giuseppe et al., 2016; Nolet, 2013). However, according to Wals (2009), the extent to which environmental and sustainability education is integrated is unclear. Thus, the entirety of a holistic picture of approaches to integration could be seen as unknown.

A synthesis of literature produced by Evans et al. (2017) focuses on approaches to the integration of environmental and sustainability education in initial teacher education programs. Collectively, this body of work and additional studies folded into this literature review are reflective of a dynamic body of globally based research that is in progress. In other words, according to Evans et al. there is no current appraisal of what is being reported to determine the state of integration of SE in teacher education. Nonetheless, the results of the synthesis based on research conducted globally led to the creation of a taxonomy of four distinctive approaches to integrating sustainability into teacher education. The four approaches are the following: (1) Embedding sustainability education widely across the curriculum areas, courses, and institution; (2) Embedding sustainability education through a dedicated core/compulsory subject; (3) Embedding sustainability education through a component of a core/compulsory subject; and (4) Embedding sustainability education through a dedicated elective subject (see pp. 410–411). The review of these approaches forms the basis of this section of the literature review.

The first approach entails *embedding of sustainability education widely across the curriculum areas, courses and institution*—and reflects the most closely to a systemic way or whole school approach to integrating sustainability education. The systemic approach entails the mainstreaming of ESD. Mainstreaming of sustainability goes across the entire educational system; it is the "incorporation of ESD philosophy, content and activities within an initial teacher education system to such an extent that ESD becomes embedded within all policies and practices" (Ferreira et al., 2007, p. 226). For mainstreaming to occur, there is the notion that sustainability will be mainstreamed into teacher education through the engagement of all stakeholders (Ferreira et al., 2006; Ferreira et al., 2009; Shallcross et al., 2006). Stakeholders defined as "key agents of change across the wider teacher education systems, which are deeply involved in the process of change" (Pe'er et al., 2013, p. 144). In the whole school approach, cooperation among all stakeholders is essential to ensure not only collaboration, but that the intentions and outcomes of the process of change are relevant to all individuals involved.

The emphasis here is to integrate sustainability by moving beyond "silos" to take a holistic or more systemic approach to teaching and learning (Evans et al., 2017, p. 410; McKeown & Hopkins, 2002). For example, Collins-Figueora (2012) reported on a whole-system, cross-disciplinary approach to biodiversity education, which formed part of a larger study on biodiversity education in Jamaica. Through a biodiversity project, the author attempted to bring together educators from numerous backgrounds on biodiversity education and ESD by facilitating a workshop, which focused on infusing and integrating biodiversity concepts. The workshop created a space to form collaborations on curricula integration for teacher educators as many had to work within an atmosphere in which ESD was not a mandatory subject in their respective primary and early childhood programs. In tandem with being part of a larger study, Van Petegem, Blieck, and Boeve-De Pauw (2007) and Van Petegem et al. (2005) reported on several modes to the integration of EE in two different teacher education programs in Belgium. The aim of the integration was to increase EE in vocational secondary education in which the status of EE was weak. Some of the authors' modes of integration reflected efforts to reorient curricula, staff professional development, and greening initiatives across the teacher education institutions.

The second approach illustrates *embedding sustainability education through a SE dedicated core/compulsory subject*. This approach, according to Evans et al. (2017) is unusual. Studies conducted in Australia by Nielson et al. (2012) and Burke and Cutter-Mackenzie (2010) both utilized experiential and place-based pedagogical approaches to the development and integration of an ESD/EE subject-based semester long course/unit. The authors of both studies created their courses with the intention of drawing connections between the subject matter and the daily lives of the students enrolled in the courses.

The third approach entails *embedding sustainability education into a component of a core/compulsory subject*. In contrast to the second approach, this is the most common. As Evans et al. (2017) note the most common modes of embedding SE into a component of a core/compulsory subject is through workshops, lectures, seminars, projects and/or online resources (e.g. Ahlberg et al., 2005, based in Finland; Jenkins, 1999/2000, based in Australia; Nelson, 2010, based in the United States; Papadimitriou, 1996, based in Greece).[6] There are additional modes such as through assessment tasks that vary in purpose from teacher reflections on the integration of ESD in teacher education, to measuring environmental knowledge (e.g., Aleixandre & Gayoso, 1996, based in Spain; Firth & Winter, 2007, based in the United Kingdom; Karpudewan et al., 2009 based in Malaysia; Varga et al., 2007 based in Hungary). Lastly, the use of the ecological footprint calculator in O'Gorman and Davis's (2013) study based out of Australia serves as a tool to challenge preservice early childhood teachers to consider the concept of sustainability in relation to their own lifestyles.

The final approach outlined by Evans et al.'s (2017) work is *embedding sustainability education through a dedicated elective subject*. The elective courses are usually presented to students in the final year of the initial teacher education programs. Within the elective courses, integration of EE varied in scope from students being offered to participate in transformative teacher education projects that highlighted the role of teachers to be able to bring awareness of local/global issues in the classroom (Alsop et al., 2007, based in Canada, Mexico, and Peru) to community problem solving (Cheong, 2005, based in Brunei).

The studies presented through the typology of Evans et al.'s (2017) work are reflective of *how* sustainability education is being embedded in teacher education programs. These studies are interventionist in nature, meaning that the authors document their own efforts to integrate environmental and sustainability perspectives into teacher education. However, there are additional studies, which provide an overview (a description) of what is occurring in teacher education programs (Ashmann & Franzen, 2017; Buchanan, 2012; Mills & Tomas, 2013; Powers, 2004; Wilson, 2012). Collectively, the aim of these studies is to provide an overview of how EE is being integrated, and the perceptions associated with the integration of EE. The studies by Mills and Tomas (2013), Buchanan (2012) and Wilson (2012) documented the practices of teacher educators in Australia within primary education teacher education programs. The studies by Buchanan and Wilson belong to much larger research projects which examined the levels of integration of sustainability education. Results indicated that teacher educators are integrating EE through multiple modes, as in through curriculum, activity-based learning, and assessment strategies. Buchanan noted that field trips and incidental learning also played a role in how students were acquiring knowledge about sustainability issues. Ashmann and Franzen (2017), and Powers's (2004) research are based in the United States and provide an overview of the integration of environmental education in teacher education programs. Large in scope, Ashmann and Franzen's study covers 33 teacher education programs in the state of Wisconsin, and Powers's study provides insight from teacher educators across 10 states within the United States. The focus of the results from the studies is the incorporation of SE through courses and activity-based learning. More specifically, Powers's work (already more focused on methods courses in integration of EE) noted integration occurred through teaching and learning outdoors, through modeling of lessons, sharing of resources and utilizing the local community as a source of learning (as in field trips to natural areas).

CHALLENGES TO THE INTEGRATION OF ENVIRONMENTAL EDUCATION IN TEACHER EDUCATION PROGRAMS

There are complex issues around the integration of environmental and sustainability perspectives into teacher education programs. One such issue is determining where the integration should take place, for example, which specific discipline or course is considered the most appropriate framework for inclusion (Heimlich et al., 2004; Ravindranath, 2007). Heimlich et al.'s (2004) results suggest there may be a preference for placing EE in methods courses or spread over various courses in teacher education programs. However, the discipline of science is traditionally viewed as such a discipline (Van Petegem, Blieck, & Van Ongevalle, 2007). Yet, focusing on a single discipline makes grasping the interdisciplinary nature of environmental and sustainability perspectives difficult (Liu, 2009; Powers, 2004; Yavetz et al., 2009). Moreover, the institutionalizing or "silo-ing" of specializations in universities has contributed to a block of using interdisciplinary approaches (Falkenburg & Babiuk, 2014, p. 423). Finding the most appropriate place for integration is further compounded by an overall lack of preservice programs with specific concentrations on EE (Beckford, 2008; Swayze et al., 2012; Hanchet, 2010; Lin, 2002).

According to Alsop et al. (2007) working in educational systems that are restrictive to ways of thinking other than market driven policies and practices severely infringes on creating an atmosphere for teaching and learning about sustainable living. Market driven policies and practices can "systematically distract from and undermine meaningful considerations of education for a sustainable future" (p. 218). Moreover, how policies and practices are affected by wider political and institutional forces within teacher education programs can lead to EE being marginalized as a subject, to being perceived as a "frill" subject (Lin, 2002, p. 209) or considered being altogether irrelevant (Dawe et al., 2005, p. 47), and afforded a low-level status through not being a mandatory course (Heimlich et al., 2004; Lin, 2002). Therefore, these circumstances make the inclusion of EE hard to justify in teacher education programs.

There are additional constraints to integrating sustainability issues in teacher education. Research by Babiuk et al. (2010), Liu (2009), and McKeown and Hopkins (2002) indicated a lack of awareness of sustainability and its relevance to the preparation of teachers at both the administrative level and at the faculty level. There are very few studies which explore teacher educators' perceptions of sustainability (Ferreira et al., 2009), and of its educative domain of EE and EFS (Evans et al., 2012).

The lack of teacher training and professional knowledge about education for sustainable development adds to the uncertainty and affects teacher educators' self-efficacy in relation to the integration of ESD into coursework (Liu, 2009; Mills & Tomas, 2013; Van Petegem et al., 2005). Moreover, there are time constraints, funding constraints, and overloaded curricula coupled with institutional policy demands that teacher educators must navigate within teacher education faculties, which lead to a lack or a partial engagement with ESD/EE (Buchanan, 2012; Ferriera et al., 2009; Gough, 2009; Heimlich et al., 2004; Inwood et al., 2014; McKeown & Hopkins, 2002).

Leadership or the lack thereof in terms of having committed individuals or faculty members to integrate environmental and sustainability perspectives is noted as a central aspect related to programming of EE in teacher education programs (Babiuk et al., 2010; Falkenburg & Babiuk, 2014). Noted as an aspect greatly needed to propel integration (Mills & Tomas, 2013), the task of leadership may be driven because of an individual or individuals with a particular interest or dedication to integration, as opposed to integration being driven by widespread integration and institutionalization of EE (McKeown-Ice, 2000; Steele, 2010).

From the review of literature, there is momentum toward the incorporation of food studies within environmental education research. This momentum is based upon the authors' recognition and response to calls for increased environmental awareness regarding food-related aspects, which are often part of larger sustainability discourses (Barth et al., 2016), and the potential of education to address these issues (Evans, 2012). Collectively, the research presented resonates a sense of urgency to address these pressing issues through education and reflect the efforts of the authors to conduct sustainability-related research (largely on an individual basis) rather than through concerted efforts (as in whole school approaches) to impact change through integration.

Moreover, this review of the literature indicates there is room for further research to take place on the overall status of integration practices on the topic of food security in environmental education occurring globally. The status of research on the intersection of food studies and EE, and on the two studies geared specifically toward teacher education programs, present an opportunity for further research in the broad field of EE. These approaches are not geared toward how the topic of food security specifically could be implemented in teacher education programs, but are nonetheless useful as starting points toward mapping out integration practices of the topic of food security. I hope that my work contributes to building an account of how integration practices are unfolding in teacher education programs in Ontario, Canada.

ENDNOTES

1. Committee on World Food Security (CFS) is an international and intergovernmental platform for all stakeholders to work together to ensure food security and nutrition for all (see http://www.fao.org/cfs/home/about/en/).
2. Hunger is generally understood when an individual has uncomfortable or painful experiences by not consuming enough food—essentially food deprivation. Malnutrition, on the other hand is a result of overall imbalance in the consumption of nutrients—either through an excess or deficiency (FAO, 2008).
3. Access is the main cause in general to food insecurity; however, the issue is still context specific. For instance, in sub-Saharan Africa chronic hunger is due to low production (Ingram, 2011, p. 418).

4. For further information on the launch of the first "Food Policy for Canada," refer to Food Secure Canada at https://foodsecurecanada.org/first-national-food-policy-for-canada
5. For De Schutter's full report access http://www.srfood.org/images/stories/pdf/officialreports/20121224_canadafinal_en.pdf
6. The notation of the countries after the date of the study is to indicate the location in which the study or research was conducted by the author.

CHAPTER 3

THEORIZING HOW TO INTEGRATE THE TOPIC OF FOOD SECURITY IN TEACHER EDUCATION

The concept of EcoJustice as will be shown below is about creating "just or equitable conditions with respect to ecological sustainability and protection of the environment, as well as social and economic issues" (Oxford Online English Dictionary, n.d.). EcoJustice in education advances a notion that the problems we, as individuals, face today are created, and maintained through our thinking and ways of being and doing that are set in the past. The patterns within our thinking, according to Bowers (2001a), Martusewicz et al. (2011) and Shiva (2005) have shaped and continue to shape relationships with ourselves, with others, and with all living things. Moreover, this theory maintains that our thinking and actions are exhibited through the language we use daily. The relevance of employing this theory to understand how to collectively move forward toward addressing issues of food security and food insecurity is to understand the thinking which underpins our actions or future actions. As the literature review on the topic of food security and food systems illustrate, some of the current solutions put forth to address these issues are in fact causing other problems such as environmental degradation—therefore, what is called for is a need for

Educating About/for Food Security Through Environmental Education: An Account of Integration Practices in Teacher Education Programs Across Ontario, Canada, pp. 37–52
Copyright © 2025 by Information Age Publishing
www.infoagepub.com
All rights of reproduction in any form reserved.

new ways of thinking leading to new actions (or solutions). For instance, understanding how the concept of food security is conceived of—that is, if the concept is seen as having a multitude of intersecting factors, or because of only a singular factor (e.g., access to food). Moreover, understanding the linkages and connections of the concept of food security allows for a potential redirection of thinking, actions and language use about the concept. These aspects of the theory are foundational to the teaching of the topic in and through educational systems, and in particular, teacher education systems.

There are several aspects that informed a conceptualization of teaching possibilities of the topic of food security in this context, which will be outlined below along with what EcoJustice Education means and what this form of education seeks to attain. These aspects are the following: (a) the role language plays in one's thinking and behaviors; (b) the concept of the commons, which are central to the theory of EcoJustice (see Bowers, 2001a, 2006; Martusewicz et al., 2011; Shiva, 2005); and (c) the use of curricular development and pedagogical strategies such as community-based learning and cultural ecological analysis; and (d) fostering an understanding of issues from a global/local outlook. Moreover, these aspects intersect and run through the definition of EcoJustice utilized in this study and build a picture of a way to understand the topic of food security. Additionally, the utilization of these aspects illustrates a method of how to teach about the topic based on viewing the topic of food security as an issue of EcoJustice.

ECOJUSTICE EDUCATION

An EcoJustice perspective according to Mueller (2009) is a "perspective that addresses the confluence of social and environmental injustice, oppression for humans and nature, and ecological degradation" (p. 1033). Mueller adds the core focus of this theory is to cultivate an outlook that fosters "an understanding of the tensions between cultures (i.e., intergenerational knowledges and skills, beliefs and values, expectations and narratives) and the needs of the Earth's ecosystems" (p. 1033).

EcoJustice in education is based on the idea of teaching this emerging perspective and to also recognize that "to be human is to live engaged in a vast and complex system of life, and [that] human well-being depends on learning how to protect it" (Martusewicz & Edmundson, 2005, p. 71). Once we, as individuals, can hold this belief, we can then move toward altering our behavior through critical reflection for the aim of creating a sustainable future (Bowers, 2012a). According to Martusewicz et al. (2011, A Cultural Ecological Analysis section) thinking critically, carefully and ethically requires us to understand how our current patterns of beliefs and behaviours "lead to destructive relationships and practices" which have harmed "the natural world as well as human communities." It also means learning "to live within a personal footprint that is sustainable and globally equitable" (Junker, 2004, p. 16).

Based on the works of Bowers (e.g., 1997, 2001a, 2012a) Martusewicz et al. (2011, EcoJustice Education section), outline six elements of EcoJustice:

1. The recognition and analysis of the deep cultural assumptions underlying modern thinking that undermines local and global ecosystems essential to life;
2. The recognition and analysis of deeply entrenched patterns of domination that unjustly define people of color, women, the poor, and other groups of humans as well as the natural world as inferior and thus less worthy of life;
3. An analysis of the globalization of modernist thinking and the associated patterns of hyper consumption and commodification that have led to the exploitation of the Southern hemisphere by the North for natural and human resources;[1]
4. The recognition and protection of diverse cultural and environmental commons-the necessary interdependent relationships of humans with the land, air, water, and other species with whom we share this planet, and the intergenerational practices and relationship among diverse groups of people that do not require the exchange of money as the primary motivation and generally result in mutual aid and support;
5. An emphasis on strong Earth democracies: the idea that decisions should be made by the people who are most affected by them, that these decisions must include consideration of the right of the natural world to regenerate, and the well-being of future generations; and
6. An approach to pedagogy and curriculum development that emphasizes both deep cultural analysis and community-based learning to encompass students to identify the causes and remediate the effects of social and ecological violence in the places where they live.

As mentioned above, these elements act as an overarching framework of EcoJustice and serve as reference points for the aim of this study. There were two main goals for this study. The first was to explore how some teacher education faculties in the province of Ontario are integrating the topic of food security into their respective teacher education programs. The second was to uncover and discuss what perspectives, if any, are guiding their practices.[2] EcoJustice Education underscores the importance of understanding why things are the way they are in terms of how individuals think, act, and behave. Examining different organizational foci of teacher education programs is a way to determine whether there is an overarching framework within teacher education programs which influences or could influence the integration of the topic of food security.[3] Moreover, the idea of everything on the planet being connected in this theoretical framework informed my choice of looking across multiple subject matter curricula, and policy documents to get as holistic a picture as possible of the coverage and potential coverage of the topic of food security.

Language and Root Metaphors

According to Stanley and Young (2011), language and looking at language use is paramount to "any discussion of ecojustice" (p. 36). The relevance of exploring language is premised on an idea that the way we think is perpetuated through the language we use daily, and the language we, as individuals, use daily reflects the culture in which one belongs (Martusewicz et al., 2011; see also Bowers, 2001b). As an individual engages in new experiences, the language of the culture acts as a lens encoded with preunderstandings that filters an interpretation of this new experience (Bowers & Flinders, 1990, p. 32). How people use language that is passed down "determines the way their relationships are created and maintained" (Lowenstein et al., 2010, p. 101). As we use language, it can also reveal our taken-for-granted assumptions. Taken for granted assumptions are the ideas that we take to be true, with no need to question or think about them.

A way to reveal these taken for granted assumptions is to understand the "metaphorical nature of language, as well as the role metaphors play in the thought process" (Bowers & Flinders, 1990, p. 33) that form the basis of the assumptions we hold to be true of the world. These assumptions are upheld by root metaphors as "the ideological sources from which the culture draws strength and reproduces itself inter-generationally" (Martusewicz et al., 2011, Root Metaphors and Discourses of Modernity section; also see Bowers, 2001b). Root metaphors provide an interpretative framework that creates and shapes how we see the world, and they can relate to specific cultural experiences and/or represent, serve and legitimate a dominant view or narrative of the world (Bowers & Flinders, 1990; Martusewicz et al., 2011). Identifying and naming root metaphors requires the understanding that words have meaning, and have a history, as well as the idea that while words can illuminate meaning, they can also hide meaning (Bowers & Flinders, 1990; Martusewicz et al., 2011).

For instance, the root metaphor of commodification (see below) as exemplified through looking at land as property and living creatures as profit underpins the idea that living things and relationships can be bought and sold. This example poses an interpretation of living things reflective of a certain way of conceiving the world brought out through language patterns. The example of commodification of living things could be considered an interpretation that skews or hides alternative interpretations of living things based on political, ethical, and social aspects of understanding this particular form of reality. Adapted from the works, for example, of Bowers, (1997, 2001a, 2006, 2012a) and Martusewicz et al. (2011, Discourses of Modernity section, para. 2 and Discourse and the Processes of Centric thinking) is an outline of root metaphors of modernity:

- **Mechanism:** sees world and life processes as being like a machine, exhibited in such terms as "information processing and "feedback systems."
- **Individualism:** an individual is seen as the basic social unit, free from culture and tradition or struggling to escape them. Exhibited in such terms as "be creative" and "think for yourself."
- **Anthropocentrism:** sees humans as the center and dominant over the rest of nature. Ignores consequences of human activity. Exhibited in such terms as "natural resources."
- **Change/Progress:** seen as linear and usually progressive, but irresistible regardless. Exhibited in such terms, "you can't stop progress," and in assumptions that "newer is better," experimenting on nature is good.
- **Science:** is seen as the most legitimate way of knowing, objective and culture free: separate from morality. Reductionist—analyzes complex phenomena by breaking into parts. Knowledge is only high status if it is derived from rational thought and formal schooling.
- **Commodification**: turning everything into a product for sale on the market. Expressed in the idea that "education is an investment in the future."
- **Consumerism:** faith in accumulation of objects as the path to happiness.
- **Androcentrism:** placing men and/or masculine point of view at the center of one's world. Men are seen as more valuable and superior to women because men hold the natural capacity to reason.
- **Ethnocentrism:** putting some cultures or groups of people at the center as more valuable than and superior to others. (Discourses of Modernity section, para. 2 and Discourse and the Processes of Centric Thinking section)

As mentioned above, these ways of thinking have become taken for granted ways of being and doing in the world that often turn into forms of engagement that are destructive to the planet. Current ways of engaging with the planet are perpetuated through societal organizations (Bowers, 2006). For example, public educational institutions, according to Bowers (2006) serve as vehicles, which transfer societal ideals into the classroom. The transferring of ideologies plays an influential role in how and what individuals learn about their relationships to self, others, and to all the communities in which they are connected. Often, and not even within the conscious realms of thought and action, educators and educational systems can reinforce destructive ways of being toward the planet.

The language patterns used within the classroom are fundamental in altering and creating worldviews and actions toward change. Changing the dominant patterns of thinking that are destructive to the planet is vital because of the role that these patterns have in influencing what is marginalized by our language and subsequently our thinking (Lupinacci, 2013, p. 190). According to Bowers (1993) "the process of schooling as well as other sources of socialization can help establish connectedness and interdependency as a more accurate way of understanding the person-community-human-natural community relationship" (p. 181). This potentiality could contribute to an alternative framework, one that works toward addressing the issue of long-term sustainability (Bowers, 1993).

The metaphorical constructs that are shaped in and through an individual's socializing process acts as a map of how the world is viewed and internalized. The map, which serves as a representation of the thoughts or metaphorical constructions, reflects a reality or territory of understanding that is communicated through language. The map-territory metaphor itself comes from the work of Gregory Bateson (1972). Bateson's explanation is that our thought processes are relational, in the way that information is communicated.

The process of receiving information is not linear, meaning that information goes from a sender to a receiver. Rather, it is a system in which the person's thought processes are constantly in motion, receiving different bits of information. The bits of information can be from what you see, hear and feel, for instance, that can affect how one processes information, and then how one subsequently goes on to understand an aspect of reality. Every bit of information that an individual encounters or experiences transforms or changes what is processed by the individual. The person is only one part of the information exchange as human thought processes are all connected rather than fragmented because they exist in an ecology—in a system of relational information exchange. As a person's thought processes take shape over time, they become a compilation of understanding or making sense of an experience. This compilation is what is referred to as a map—the mental metaphorical constructs, and these maps shape how the territory—the domains of information such as an event, or relationship (within a cultural and/or natural system or both) are recognized. To clarify, what is not included in a person's map may often go unnoticed; the map itself may have an inadequate (not a full) representation of the territory of experience (Bateson, 1972, pp. 455–460). In other words, the territory may not represent what is currently occurring in a cultural and/or natural system (e.g., current occurrences in parts of the world, and species near extinction, etc.). The processing of information in the form of an individual's "thought, awareness and source of meaning" are influenced by language use, that is the language used by the individual reflects how the individual interprets the experience (Bowers, 2012b, p. 25). Moreover, the language is based on the metaphorical maps which one uses to "describe and understand the external world" (Bowers, 2012b, p. 25). The problem Bateson sees when addressing environmental issues for instance, is if one uses the same language (based on metaphorical maps) of a territory (also based or conceived as unchanging) from the past to address issues in the present, then the same types of issues can continue. Given this line of thinking, one can rewrite one's map of understanding, and take on new ways of engaging with the world (Bowers, 2012b; Lupinacci, 2013).

Just as there are identified root metaphors which are seen as destructive to the planet, there are root metaphors of sustainable cultures. Grounded in the works of Bowers (e.g., 1997, 2001a, 2012a) and Martusewicz et al. (2011) outline a list of root metaphors shared by societies which are seen as more sustainable:

- **Holistic/organic:** sees the world as interconnected like a living thing. Views humans and the rest of nature in reciprocal relationship of interdependence.
- **Community-centered:** sees community as a basic social unit. Elders conserve and pass on traditions that sustain community and ecology. Community includes the rest of nature.
- **Ecocentric:** sees humans and other life and non-living as equal participants in a moral universe. Humans have a moral obligation to nature.
- **Controlled change:** Stability is valued. All cultures change, but here, change is evaluated in terms of long-term consequences. Past and future are important considerations in decisions.
- **Science:** is just one-way of knowing. Science is holistic, focusing on whole systems rather than parts, on understanding relationships and patterns. Knowledge comes in many forms—tacit, folk, poetic, spiritual, technical, encoded in language, genes, plants.

- **Non-commodified**: traditions are maintained based on intrinsic value and meaning. Markets and monetary transactions are a small part of culture. (Discourse and the Processes of Centric Thinking section)

To reiterate, striving to identify and deconstruct root metaphors works in tandem with Bowers's (1997, 2001a, 2012a) definition of EcoJustice. Thus, learning to recognize the ways of thinking and behaving that have a negative impact on our communities, can be shifted to an alternate relationship based on ways of thinking and being that create and foster just and sustainable communities (Martusewicz & Edmundson, 2005).

The idea of "thinking" having an impact upon "action" toward food and food production is shown through an example of increasing foodstuffs for some of the world's most food insecure people, but not realizing that continuing this same path of using technological methods (known to be problematic) will only exacerbate the problem. These high yielding methods are referred to as productivist methods premised on cultural notions (of modernist thinking) of efficiency and high quantity. But these methods are also noted to cause biodiversity loss, and soil erosion (Foresight, 2011, as cited in Maye & Kirwan, 2013; Gardner, 2013; Ingram, 2011; Sage, 2012). The result is the fixing of one problem of not having enough food amounts, to the creation of new ones that then perhaps may require another technological fix to solve. This situation is reflective of what David Orr (2011) calls fast knowledge. Fast knowledge is based on the idea that solutions to problems are created with the idea that technological advances are solutions to problems in relationship to the environment (Orr, 2011, Chapter 2, para. 3, 5). In other words, fast knowledge applications to solving problems creates band-aid solutions to current problems predicated on the misuse of language. As a result of language being misused—that is not understood, there is difficulty in working toward "solv[ing] problems that we cannot name" (Orr, 2011, Chapter 1, end of para. 4). What this means is that fast knowledge approaches can solve a problem quickly and even with efficiency yet leave a trail of issues created by that approach which needs to be solved. The application of a technological "fix" for every problem pushes aside ways of being and doing in the world that have survived throughout generations and that have valuable input. However, these ways of being and doing are not considered valuable in the face of technological knowledge. Therefore, there is a particular view of what is most appropriate or believed to be the most appropriate solution to the food insecurity problem.

Additionally, in trying to understand the topic of food security and insecurity and the subsequent solutions needed for sustained food security worldwide, I understand EcoJustice to offer the contention of understanding that everything is related (Martusewicz et al. 2011, see also Shiva, 2005). Thinking in this manner to move toward just and sustainable communities is about thinking that calls upon individuals to work together. The topic of food security warrants the same type of thinking to meet not only the parameters of the definition but to approach the creation of solutions in a holistic manner. By this understanding, thinking needs to be based on seeing that all aspects of the food system are connected, and this idea, in turn affects the state of food security. For instance, food waste or the increasing amount of food being wasted directly links to food supply, which in turns links to the consumer. The issue is one of food supply, food prices and food access as being interconnected (The Economist Intelligence Unit, 2014).

As I have mentioned, the topic of food security and EcoJustice hold many points of alignment that underscore ways of thinking toward the planet. The suitability of EcoJustice Education as a theoretical framework for understanding and building knowledge and awareness about the topic of food security is evident as EcoJustice pushes all members of society to reconsider how they engage with each other and with the planet daily. EcoJustice is useful in understanding issues pertinent to creating a state of food security given that how food is understood and perceived influences (determines) the ways in which it is produced, distributed, and consumed. Similarly, EcoJustice Education is asking us to understand that how one sees oneself in relation to all living things affects one's relationship to all living things. Some of the effects of the globalized food system are in fact side-effects of the initial ways of thinking, such as in the separation between humans, and all living processes exhibited through a loss of biodiversity and increases in food waste (Shiva, 2005, 2013; Vivero-Pol, 2014).

In the next section, I take up the concepts of the commons and enclosure in relation to the commons. These aspects of the theoretical framework as well as the discussion on language and root metaphors, form the basis used in pedagogy and curriculum development discussed after the following section.

Commons, Commons Thinking, and Enclosure

The concept of the commons defined by Shiva (2005), "implies a resource is owned, managed, and used by the community" (p. 21). In other words, the commons represent what has not been altered into market relationships—meaning that the "life sustaining and life enhancing resources and services that have not been divided up and assigned a monetary value in the global economy, but instead are shared—according to evolving arrangements and agreements—among members of a community or group" (Kendrick, 2009, p. 51). The commons are comprised of physical systems as well as the cultural commons. The physical commons (also referred to as natural or environmental) are composed of shared aspects such as land, air, water and all living creatures on the planet. The cultural commons are formed by cultural patterns, traditions, practices and rituals of a community. This type of commons is seen through the arts, intergenerational knowledge sharing, mentoring relationships within the community, information, language, food cultivation, and preparation skills. The cultural commons are largely non-monetized, rather than monetized exchanges amongst community members (Bowers, 2006, 2012a, Appendix B; Martusewicz et al., 2011; Shiva, 2005). Moreover, in order to continue and enhance the cultural commons, they are relational and are formed by democratic participation, and "social relations based on interdependence, and cooperation" (Shiva, 2005, p. 21).

EcoJustice educators advance the notion of creating new ways of being and doing in the world. To begin to accomplish this notion, teaching involves the "recognition and re-valuing [of] diverse commons-based practices, traditions and knowledge from cultures and communities worldwide" (Lowenstein et al., 2010, p. 103). Mueller (2009) states to develop an understanding of the tensions between cultures and the Earth's ecosystems, there needs to be the cultivation of a worldview that strikes to balance and protect the environment while ensuring the well-being of all. Moreover, with all the planet's living beings connected and sharing commonalties, we need to find a way to acknowledge these commonalities and protect them in order to survive. Examining how the various types of commons operate within one's own community allows for an evaluation of current practices built on an industrial/consumerist lifestyle with existing skills and talents inherent in the communities that form the basis of support systems. Working toward protecting the commons is the basis and argument toward achieving sustainability and social justice (Bowers, 2006, 2012a; Shiva, 2005).

However, the commons can become enclosed. Enclosure is defined as the transformations of aspects of a culture, and of the Earth's resources that were once freely shared by members of the community, in an attempt to appropriate, own and sell these resources. In turn, collective decision-making becomes secondary to privatized, individualized and/or corporatized management of the commons. The mentality of enclosure is based on a way of thinking or perceiving of the world that places humans, and human-related activities as separate and above the Earth, rather than part of a collectivity. In addition, the mentality of enclosure produces a mindset that persuades and reinforces one to act in their interests, that is the inclination toward individualism, instead of togetherness based on commonalities. Through this thinking, the commons continue to become commoditized, sold as goods and services of which the consumer has little control over, either in terms of quality, price and/or decision-making (Bowers, 2009a; Kendrick, 2009; Ricoveri, 2013; Shiva, 2005).

To restore the imbalance that has occurred and continues to occur from the enclosure of the commons, our thinking needs to shift away from individualism to one based on fortifying and maintaining our commonalities (Kendrick, 2009; Shiva, 2005). Both Kendrick (2009) and Shiva (2005) advance a way of thinking centered on the commons—with Kendrick utilizing the terms commons thinking, and Shiva articulating the perspective of living economies. Commons thinking "recognizes the rich resources available to us by starting from ensuring the well-being of locality, and the well-being of others in their locality" (Kendrick, 2009, p. 55). The commons way of thinking starts from an abundance perspective rather than a deficiency perspective in thinking, which requires "competition over resources made scarce by that very competition" (Kendrick, 2009, p. 55). Similarly, Shiva (2005) advances that our thinking about the earth needs to shift to facilitate living economies. Living economies are "processes and spaces where the earth's resources are shaped equitably" (p. 5), and through this equitable shaping people are able to meet their food and water needs to create and maintain fulfilling lives and livelihoods.

Undertaking the notion of living economies will require that humans view themselves as members of the Earth family. Belonging to the Earth family entails the responsibility of caring for all species and life on the planet. As humans continue to engage with the earth, it is imperative to "live, produce and consume within ecological limits, and within our share of ecological space" (Shiva, 2013, pp. 9–10). According to this perspective, these ways of thinking need to put the welfare of the earth at the centre rather than at the periphery of one's worldview. What is being stated is the notion that one's well-being depends on the well-being of all members of the planet (including non-humans), and that working from this perspective as a mode of solving problems can work to restore relationships of trust instead of the imposition of solutions upon others (Kendrick, 2009).

In relating the concept of the commons to understanding food and food security, there is a connection between the enclosure of the commons with the state of food security and/or insecurity. As mentioned above, Eco-Justice Education advances the notion that some of the problems we face today are due to the enclosure of the commons. Food, as it stands now, is commodified, bought, sold, and traded on the economic market like other items, and it is not accessible to each and every person for their survival. In other words, food is not held in common. The continuous enclosure of food further alienates people from being food secure and maintaining hunger and malnutrition. Moreover, by food being commodified, the non-economic qualities of food are marginalized (e.g., part of one's national culture) as well as the fundamental aspect of the biological necessity of food. Food is not viewed as a right given to everyone when food is commodified (Shiva, 2005; Vivero-Pol, 2014).

When food is privatized, and the means to produce food such as seeds, land and agro-chemicals are also largely privatized, there is an increase in the loss of employment for farmers, and/or food producers. If farmers do not have enough income to purchase items needed to produce food, let only sell their produce on the market in competition with other food producers, they lose their position in the economy. Moreover, if farmers are required to use patented seeds such as GMOs, the cycle of low income, and the inability to purchase required items for food production continues, with a "no money-no food rationality" (Vivero-Pol, 2014, p. 4; see also Shiva, 2005, 2013). The patterns of domination exhibited by enclosure are what EcoJustice Education is asking us to not only recognize but work toward changing through building new understandings of the commons, and/or revitalizing what already exists that works toward sustainable communities.

Thus far, the concepts discussed from the theoretical framework, and the application of the theory to my study, establish the discussion in the following section. In the next section, I outline pedagogical and curricular approaches which emphasize the use of community-based learning, cultural ecological analysis and developing a global/local understanding of an issue.

Approaches to Teaching and Learning

The focus of the approaches discussed here illustrates an integration of the concepts outlined above, as to how the concepts could be incorporated into the educational system. The application of learning about the commons in an educational setting can be done through community-based learning (Dallimore et al., 2010) whereby teachers and students can learn about the commons through understanding the places in which they live (Lowenstein et al., 2010). This type of teaching engages multiple individuals and perspectives, such as faculty, community members and students working in tandem to meet goals set out by an educational institution and the community (Bortolin, 2013; Dallimore et al., 2010). This approach to teaching and learning is also based on the ideas that all communities have inherent educational resources and points of interest that can enhance learning experiences for students. The appeal of this approach is that student learning is based on real-life issues, is focused on building problem-solving skills, and can foster civic action on the part of students to address issues in their communities (Smith & Sobel, 2010). According to Bortolin (2013), community-based learning is "a fusion of theory and practice" (p. 27) and folds together classroom-based learning styles with activities based on experience at the community level. From the broad understanding of community-based learning, other terms, such as place-based education (Gruenewald & Smith, 2008; Smith & Sobel, 2010), service learning (Bringle & Hatcher, 1996; Melaville et al., 2006), experiential learning (Dewey, 1974; Lewis & Williams, 1994) and community-based research (Strand et al., 2003) are sometimes used interchangeably, or with community based-learning. However, the usage of a particular term is dependent on the context and purposes in which it is used, such as in the *focus* of a certain project (Bortolin, 2013; Melaville et al., 2006). For instance, place-based education is generally understood to use the student's local environment—the unique historical, environmental, cultural, and economic traits as a source of teaching and learning. The focus of the student's work is directed toward the community's interests and needs, and community members are part of the learning and teaching process for students as they serve as resources and partners (Gruenewald & Smith, 2008; Smith & Sobel, 2010). In contrast, the term service learning or community service learning is an academic experience in which students participate in an academic project that is to provide a service to the community and to meet the needs of the community. Moreover, this activity provides the opportunity for students to reflect on the service activity, to learn more in depth about the content of the course, to deepen a sense of civic responsibility, and to fortify and strengthen communities (Bringle & Hatcher, 1996; Melaville et al., 2006).

Experiential learning is learning that occurs by doing or learning from experience. This form of learning is based on having students immersed in an experience, followed by reflection about the experience. The purpose of reflection is to "develop new skills, new attitudes, or new ways of thinking" (Lewis & Williams, 1994, p. 5). Community-based research, according to Strand et al. (2003) refers to a collaborative partnership of students, faculty and community-based members who together conduct research with the intention of addressing and solving a pressing issue within the community or to cause social change. As evidenced, the various terms have a commonality in the forms of learning that promote engagement by the student—meaning the student is not a bystander of the learning. Instead, the student is part of the learning that is to take place through the specific foci of the project or work to be done by the student.

Within the context of this theory, community-based learning sets out to engage students through the following steps: (1) Identify serious problems in their communities; (2) Analyze the roots of those problems in larger socioeconomic and cultural systems; and (3) Create localized, healthy relationships with mentors and with each other in the context of our immediate ecosystems (Lowenstein et al., 2010, p. 103). Both students and teachers are vital to the learning process and are asked to work together to recognize and work with the communities' assets in which they live. Working together encourages the utilization of intergenerational knowledge and skills held by community members that could serve to help analyze and solve problems within the community. Community-based learning experiences framed by EcoJustice underscore the importance of getting both students and teachers to understand the root issues that have caused harmful practices and disconnections to members and between members of communities in which they live (Lowenstein et al., 2010; Martusewicz et al., 2011). As this process unfolds, Bowers (2009a) believes this learned understanding of the local and environmental commons inherent to the places in which one lives, could cause one to strive to protect or in fact change the patterns of behaviors present in those places which augment harm to these places.

As learning is contextualized for students, through an engagement with places, people, ecosystems, and living creatures, teachers can help facilitate learning that draws students' attention and awareness to the idea that all living creatures are interconnected. While participating in these learning experiences outside of the classroom, students are offered the opportunity to work toward creating solutions and are positioned to consider themselves as part of the community to which they belong, as well as see that their participation in the community is seen as vital and necessary (Bowers, 1993; Lowenstein et al., 2010).

In conjunction with the emphasis on community-based learning, cultural ecological analysis is also utilized within this framework. Before moving on to what a cultural ecological analysis is, I explain what is meant by the words cultural and ecological in the context of this theory. The term culture, as discussed by Martusewicz et al. (2011), "is a very malleable and fluid set of meanings and relationships, created as people engage and interact and communicate with one another" (Cultural Foundations of the Crisis section, para 5). Cultural systems (upon which the analysis is trying to unpack) are created by "maps" (as mentioned above) that become part of our daily thinking. Ecological refers to human communities as being "nested within ecological systems" (On Difference, Intelligence, and an "Ecology of Mind," para. 1), and ecological as a term is referenced as the "idea of human relationships to other living systems as a living, communicating, and generative whole, all set within a limited Earthly context" (On Difference, Intelligence, and an "Ecology of Mind," para. 2). Thus, cultural ecological analysis is the development of the understanding that both the ecological and social issues currently facing our world have cultural assumptions about certain ways of being and doing formed by modernist thinking (Martusewicz et al., 2011). As a result of the presence of this way of thinking, enacting a cultural ecological analysis is about fostering a different way of thinking about relationships individuals have with each other, and the natural world. It is about assisting learners in developing ways of thinking that are critical and mindful, as well as ethical. Focusing on such a task is about unpacking the "patterns of beliefs and behaviour in our culture that have led to destructive relationships and practices harming the natural world as well as human communities" (Martusewicz et al., 2011, A Cultural Ecological Analysis section, para. 1). Using this process is based on pulling from multidisciplinary backgrounds, for instance, philosophical analysis, sociology of knowledge, and sociolinguistics (to a name a few) (see Cultural Foundations of the Crisis section). The purpose is to recognize and draw out how it is that we, as individuals, have developed the way we think in this present culture (Martusewicz et al., 2011, p. 50). A direct way to uncover this thinking is by analyzing the language used on a daily basis. The analysis of language with aspects such as root metaphors (discussed above) can illustrate how humans make meaning from the words used to convey an aspect of reality. Additionally, this process can show how humans use language to create relationships with all living things, but also the impact of this thinking upon these relationships (Bowers, 2001a; Martusewicz et al., 2011).

Building an awareness and understanding toward a global/local outlook in teaching for EcoJustice is premised on several of the ideas mentioned above. That is, fostering a global/local outlook in understanding an issue is about creating learning opportunities for students to grasp the linkages that exist in the world which show the world to be connected. The (inter) connectedness or (inter) linkages between places can result in occurrences that happen in one part of the world, which affect another part of the world. In essence, EcoJustice educators want students to grasp the idea of the global/local interconnectedness, the effects of the global/local interconnections, and to understand the reason behind the global/local interconnections and effects.

Teaching and learning in and through an understanding of EcoJustice for a food secure world, asks for a peeling back of our taken for granted assumptions about how food is produced, and who the production affects, for instance (Martusewicz et al., 2011; Shiva, 2013). Moreover, it asks us to recognize why and how things are the way they are, in order to shift the current reality and to create new possibilities. EcoJustice Education envisions the goals of schooling to not reproduce cultural assumptions that further divide all species, but to teach in a way that fosters a sense of responsibility based on just and ethical obligations to the communities to which we belong (Martusewicz et al., 2011).

ENDNOTES

1. Modernist thinking is a way of understanding and conceiving of the world as being one based on hierarchized relationships. Hierarchized relationships

are relationships that are seen to have more value than others, such as the idea that certain humans have more value over other humans, and over living things (Lowenstein et al., 2010).
2. Throughout this study I use the term perspective by which I am referring to the type(s) of root metaphor shown within the integration practices of the participants and documents.
3. By overarching framework, I am referring to a framework that shapes the overall focus of what a program wants to address, as in raising awareness of oppression, for instance.

CHAPTER 4

THE STUDY

QUALITATIVE RESEARCH DESIGN

This study utilized a qualitative descriptive research approach because through qualitative research there is importance placed upon the quality of the processes and meaning of experiences, instead of emphasis placed upon "measurement and analysis of casual relationships between variables within the data (Denzin & Lincoln, 2011, p. 8). The importance of processes and meanings as a focal point of qualitative research met the aim of this study through focusing upon documenting integration practices by teacher education programs, and on the perspectives contained within the documents as well as held by teacher educators about the concept of food security. Qualitative research also aligned with the theoretical framing of EcoJustice Education used for this study, in that the theory calls for building an understanding of how people conceive of an issue, and how the various conceptualizations held by people in this case teacher educators influenced their integration practices, as well as why certain strategies of integration were used.

Upon designing this study, I considered the notion that teacher education programs can acts as bounded systems within universities. Bounded systems, according to Stake (2009) are unit(s) around which there are boundaries to assist in delineating the scope of a study. Teacher educators work within a larger system that is mediated by factors outside of

---

Educating About/for Food Security Through Environmental Education: An Account of Integration Practices in Teacher Education Programs Across Ontario, Canada, pp. 53–67
Copyright © 2025 by Information Age Publishing
www.infoagepub.com
All rights of reproduction in any form reserved.

their own pedagogical and curricular methods. For instance, studies within teacher education and environmental education indicate that teacher educators struggle to implement issues around the environment and sustainability due to lack of priority, opportunity, and levels of commitment from teachers to the alignment of interests and commitment in programs and institutional policy (Babiuk et al., 2010; Ferreira et al., 2009).

Acknowledging the existence of issues that relate to the integration of EE mentioned above, I sought to collect data that could assist in determining if there are similar issues towards the integration of the topic of food security in select teacher education programs. As part of determining if there are similar issues as outlined in the literature review within the data, I used the understanding of integration based on Evans et al.'s (2017) call for integration of sustainability to occur in a systemic way. A systemic approach to integration of sustainability means the concept of sustainability becomes a core focus—that is the concept is "included as an integral part of the school/departmental policies, core foci, daily practices and activities" (p. 410). In this study, I analyzed the data collected to determine if integration of the topic of food security occurred in this manner across the teacher education systems investigated. Moreover, the chosen theory of EcoJustice Education used for this study supports the notion of a systemic approach to integration which allows for building an understanding of food security to be done in an interrelated and coordinated effort, which in turn means the topic is integrated across a "whole-of-program" (p. 410). In this case, the building of such an understanding of the topic of food security is by using specific teaching strategies, the analysis of perspectives embedded within integration, and the use of cross-curricular delivery of subject matter content. A push for such an approach to education is based on David Orr's (2011) notion that "all education is environmental education" (Chapter 26, Ecological Literacy, para 12). Therefore, the integration of the topic of food security needs to be woven across all educational opportunities.

The data collected for this study assisted in contributing to understanding how integration is unfolding in teacher education programs[1] in terms of the topic of food security. The data collected were the following: (1) Documents from each faculty of education (teacher education program) as in course descriptions, program overviews, and teacher educators' syllabi; (2) Ontario Ministry of Education curriculum and policy documents; and (3) Interviews with teacher educators within select faculties of education. Through the collection of these types of data determining opportunities for integration could occur, and could provide feedback on interest, commitment, and policy directions in programs. Additionally, the intention behind the collection of these data types is that they would provide a snapshot of current integration practices on the topic of food security within select teacher education programs in Ontario.

The selection of Ontario as the site of my study is based on the characteristics of the province that allow for a plausible study of teaching and learning about/for the topic of food security. Ontario is a highly urbanized province with more than 80% of the population living in urban areas, and with a total population of around 14,223,942 (Statistics Canada, 2022). This percentage corresponds to Canada's population, whereby the majority of Canadians live in urban areas totaling 81.56% (Trading Economics, 2022). The highlighting of urban populations in relation to discussing food security and/or food insecurity, for instance, rests on the notion that as the world population continues to grow, it is projected to move into urban areas.[2] Although moving into urban areas could provide various benefits, such as increased opportunities (e.g., employment), this is not always the case (Cohen & Garrett, 2009). As more people are expected to move into urban areas that means there is the need to provide more food goods and services to cities—as well as the fact that people moving into urban areas need to know how to access these services including living (preferably) within locations that are close to supermarkets to purchase food (see Dieterle, 2015, for a discussion on food deserts).

Researcher Positionality

As a researcher, it is imperative to reflect upon my own bias, personal position and conflict of interest in regard to the participants and the topic of this study. Given the topic of food insecurity and the environment are highly complex, sensitive and personalized areas of understanding and experience, I held to the role of a researcher acting as a mediator of understanding (Bowers, 2004). I understand this role to mean that I, as the researcher, am not the holder of all knowledge and experience on these topics but rather there to gather insights, engage in deep conversation and reflection with participants. While I have not claimed to be the holder of knowledge on this topic, I do believe that by recognizing and understanding the ways in which my thoughts, values and experiences of the issue of food insecurity may have affected this research I have minimized bias in my findings.

As an educator who has taught in various classrooms, I have seen much diversity within the student population and have witnessed several implementations of food security programs. Given this experience, I have come to adopt a view of what food security or insecurity could look like and how it affects the daily learning of students. Additionally, through familial experiences of food insecurity, there is a collected understanding of emotions and thoughts that resonate within my own personal conceptualization of this imperative issue—I state personal here because food security/insecurity is a highly contextualized experience. With this understanding of the issue, I did not ask any interview questions to my participants that related to explaining personal examples or situations of food insecurity of themselves or others to garner information about how this topic is understood. In terms of interviewing participants, I tried to make participants feel as comfortable as possible by allowing pauses between questions, and/or having participants come back to questions that may have been difficult to answer at the onset. Through ongoing conversation with participants before and during the interviews I reiterated that although there exist multiple definitions of food security/insecurity, the definitions, understandings and conceptualizations shared through their participation are of equal value to building an understanding of this topic and towards creating a food secure world.

Through my graduate work in the areas of food security, environmental sustainability and curriculum studies in combination with my personal experiences I have formed particular views about how I believe the issue should be dealt with and learned about from the standpoint of an educator, academic and citizen. However, I was very diligent and conscientious about reflecting the complexity of the topic of food security/insecurity through compiling academic literature that spanned various subject matter disciplines. The literature review for this study reflects the complexities of the topic, which further confirms that the topic is understood and dealt with from a myriad of standpoints. By researching, reviewing and organizing the literature in this manner, I believe that I have lessened my personal bias as much as possible and provided a detailed and broader review of the topic.

Selection of Sites and Participants

In this study, my selection of faculties of education was purposeful (Merriam, 2009). The first criteria for the selection of faculties was to select faculties that ranged from organizational focus to see the relationship between the framing of the program and the actual practices within the program. I scanned teacher education programs online prior to contact, to profile the nature of the programs offered. The range was based on: (1) programs with an explicit organizational focus on environmental education, (2) programs with an explicit organizational focus on social justice and not an explicit focus on environmental education, and (3) programs which do not state an explicit focus on either environmental education or social justice.

The participants recruited within the teacher education programs were professors (both full-time and part-time) who have been present within the faculty for at least three years. The reasoning behind this selection was to have participants who could have the opportunity within their respective teacher education programs to integrate the topic. In other words, having a participant with these criteria could potentially result in a participant being able to integrate the topic and note and discuss successes and challenges to integration. Participants were primarily recruited through email, as well as through face-to-face invitation at a national education conference.

For the recruitment and selection of participants, I tried to ensure as much variation as possible in perspectives of integration and of teaching practices. Therefore, I did not limit my selection to any one specific subject area domain of research (e.g., Social Studies or Science). Rather, I sought to include potential participants who had the following criteria: (1) State they work on the topic of food/food security; (2) State they work on the topic of environmental education and sustainability, and social justice; (3) State they work with related topics such as science, technology, social studies, health and physical education, Indigenous studies, and interdisciplinary studies. In essence, I was trying to align the content area of the curriculum documents with the recruitment of content-based teaching or methods courses. The reasoning behind seeking a variation of perspectives displays a purposeful selection of participants in that the variation could help fill this aim within my study (Guest et al., 2013). This point aligns with scholars working within the fields of food security and foods systems writ large as well as with my chosen theoretical framework of EcoJustice Education and in the field of EE. These research areas advance the need to create a holistic and/or interdisciplinary understanding of the issues that affect food security and environmental and sustainability issues (Allen, 2013; Ardoin et al., 2012; Martusewicz et al., 2011).

The goal of the purposeful selection was to get at how participants describe the teaching of the content of the topic of food security, as well as whether the organizational focus of a teacher education program allows for (or not) the integration of the topic of food security. I was interested in seeing in what ways is integration of the topic of food security in teacher education programs in Ontario occurring and what perspectives are guiding these integration practices.

DATA COLLECTION

This research utilized both document reviews and semi-structured interviews. There are several types of documents collected for this study that are from the teacher education programs of which the participants were interviewed as well as various Ontario Ministry of Education curriculum documents (elementary and secondary levels), and other related policy and/or initiatives. The latter data were analyzed prior to the recruitment stage (this examination corresponds to the stage of the data analysis phase). A detailed description of the various data collected are outlined below.

Program Overviews, Course Descriptions, and Professors' Syllabi. In online form, I collected teacher education program overviews to review the established objectives set out for each program. Within the programs, I compiled course descriptions that students are offered as part of the program. This data assisted in providing insight into the current opportunities that exist for teaching about/for food security. Keeping this data in mind, I cross-checked professors' course syllabi to determine how the participants have negotiated or mediated the established objectives of the teacher education program, and the objectives of the course descriptions through the creation of course syllabi.

Background on Teacher Educators. *Participants' Characteristics.* Table 4.1 illustrates characteristics of participants collected through syllabi, online program searches and interviews in each of the respective faculties of education.

Chart on Environmental Education Courses in Teacher Education Programs. The compiled chart is listed as Appendix E. The rationale for the inclusion of the chart is to show which faculties of education have in place a course on environmental education as a potential option for integration of the topic of food security.

Ontario Ministry of Education Documents: Curriculum and Policy Documents and Health Canada Teacher Resource. The choice of selecting curriculum documents as a form of data is based on the idea that curriculum and policy documents shape common curriculum (Auger & Rich, 2007), that is "what students must know and be able to do at the end of every grade or course in every subject," as stated by the Ontario Ministry of Education (2019, Frequently Asked Questions section). My goal was to find out what is the common content on the topic of food security in the curriculum documents. I was interested in examining the content contained within various subjects to determine the amount and extent of coverage on the topic of food security as is—meaning the content contained within them in the form that the information is presented (this is before teacher implementation in the classroom). Moreover, because the curriculum documents are developed and reviewed by individuals with diverse backgrounds (e.g. experts in subject disciplines across the province), as well as the curriculum review process being a "research-based and evidence-informed process" (Ontario Ministry of Education, 2019, Frequently Asked Questions), I was interested in finding out what specific aspects and perspectives of the topic are included by the selection of curriculum content to be the knowledge that students are to acquire.

In order to find out what is contained within the Ontario Ministry of Education documents, I reviewed the following documents in the following

Table 4.1

Title: Participant Characteristics—Teacher Educators

Name of institution and participant (Pseudonyms)	Status of the participant within the faculty (Full or Part-time)	Course used in integration	Strategy used to integrate the topic within the course	Department has an EE course or related course
University of Burnaby Martin	Full time	Issues in Secondary Education How to teach for sustainability in the 21st C? (e.g. place-based, food security education)	• Professional learning community • Community service-learning project	Yes
Greenbank University Alexis	Part-time	Science (Primary/Junior) Environmental Education	• Environmental issues through science STSE strand (Science, technology, Society and Environment) • Core engagement of the class	Yes
Tulip College Stephanie	Full-time	Alternative placement (open to all students)	• Learning garden (garden-based activities)	Yes
Seedsboro University Beatrice	Full-time	Environmental Education across the curriculum	• Big Ideas (socio-economic, and environmental)	Yes
PanCanadian College Harvey	Part-time	Global Issues and Education	• In process	Yes

subject matters of *Social Studies Grades 1–6, and History and Geography Grades 7–8 (2013a), Science and Technology Grades 1–8 (2007c) and Health and Physical Education Grades 1–8 (2015b)* at the elementary level and *Social Studies and Humanities Grades 9–12 (2013b), Science Grades 9 and 10 (2008a), Grades 11 and 12 (2008b), Technological Education Grades 9 and 10 (2009a), Grades 11 and 12 (2009b), Health and Physical Education Grades 9–12 (2015), Canadian and World Studies Grades 9, and 10 (2013c), and Grades 11 and 12*

(2015a), *Native Studies Grades 9 and 10 (1999)*, and *Grades 11 and 12 (2000)* and *Interdisciplinary studies Grades 11 and 12 (2002)* at the secondary levels. The overarching rationale for the selection of these documents is threefold: (1) These specific subject content areas align with the broader research in food security and food system literature, (2) These documents capture a provincial snapshot of the current ways in which food security is being addressed through education in Ontario, and (3) Curriculum documents act as guidelines for instruction; therefore, they are resources at both the teacher education level and at the classroom level.

Additionally, the Ontario Ministry of Education's Environmental Education related documents such as *Shaping our Schools, Shaping our Future: Environmental Education in Ontario Schools (2007b)*, and *Acting Today, Shaping Tomorrow (2009c) and the Environmental Education Scope and Sequence of Expectations and the Kindergarten program 1–8 (2017b), 9–12 (2017a)* and *Ready set Green! Tips, Techniques and Resources from Ontario Educators (2007a)*, were reviewed to determine if there is any reference to a relationship of food and the environment as part of the vision of Ontario schools.

Other policy documents were collected: *Healthy Food for Healthy schools Act (2008c), School Food and Beverage Policy: Resource Guide (2010a)*, and *Policy/Program Memorandum No. 150 (2010b) and Health Canada Eating Well with Canada's Food guide (2011)*. I reviewed these documents, to decipher to what extent Ontario is addressing the connection between food and nutrition as part of one's overall food security.

Since documents convey ideologies, whether explicitly or implicitly, their applicability can be far-reaching (Savin-Baden & Howell Major, 2013). The documents collected serve as guidelines and resources for teacher educators and future classroom teachers. Therefore, analyzing these documents for ideologies they contain applies not only to the student and/or teachers but also to the wider community in advancing understandings of food security.

Interviews

The purpose of the interviews I sought to conduct was to obtain descriptions of integration practices in teacher education programs to be able to access and learn about the context of the integration practices and to really understand why teacher educators were doing what they were doing through teaching. All interviews were audio recorded and were conducted with the five-teacher educator participants and lasted for a time duration of 30–55 minutes. The different modes of interviewing were Skype and/or by phone. All participants at the end of the interviews were given an annotated bibliography on the topic of food security that I created that was sent via email.

- The data collection process emphasized the dissertation study's questions:
  a. In what ways do teacher education programs in Ontario describe the integration of the topic of food security into their programs?
  b. What pedagogical practices and curricular strategies are being utilized across teacher education programs to raise awareness and motivate action for food security?
  c. To what extent do the strategies used within teacher education programs support an EcoJustice-oriented education?
- What perspectives (root metaphors) underpin the integration of the topic of food security within teacher education programs?
  a. What implications can the perspectives have upon teacher educators' orientations toward integration, and the role of EE in addressing them?

DATA OF INTERVIEWS AND DOCUMENTS

In preparation of the data for analysis, I held as a reminder what Bowers (2012a) and Orr (2011) underscore about the importance of language, in that how we understand an issue, and how we project our thinking of an issue through language can perpetuate our treatment of the issue. As a result of this way of thinking, how something is described as through the use of metaphor can reveal not only a way of thinking but also the cultural assumptions embedded in that particular way of thinking. The purpose of the data analysis is to explore the perspectives through language used that guide the integration of the topic of food security in select teacher education programs in Ontario. The theoretical framework of EcoJustice Education chosen for my study forms a conceptualization of how to teach the topic of food security through creating ways of thinking and forms of engagement with the earth in respect to food security.

As part of data organization in both the collection and analysis, I used the qualitative data analysis software NVivo (Bazeley & Jackson, 2013). I created individual files for each teacher education program, as well as the Ontario Ministry documents, as they interact with each faculty being examined. Each faculty was examined with all the related documents before I moved on to analyze the next program. This step was done to gain as best as possible a cohesive picture for each faculty on integration. However, because there is the possibility that the content in the public documents may be mentioned in the interviews, I examined all the public documents prior to the recruitment and commencement of the interviews, for instance, the official Ontario Ministry of Education documents. The data were analyzed in two phases. Prior to the recruitment phase I conducted data analysis stage 1 of the documents (Ontario Ministry of Education curriculum and policy documents), and prior to the commencement of the interviews I conducted data analysis Stage 2 of the documents (Ontario Ministry of Education curriculum and policy documents). Moreover, I was able to collect professors' syllabi before starting the interviews, with the purpose of scanning the syllabi and using the information contained within them as points of conversation during the interviews. All interviews were transcribed, and the transcriptions were stored in the appropriate file.

To facilitate the process of identifying the ways in which the topic of food security is presented within the data, I created a numbered list of concepts on the topic of food security formed from Rocha's (2008) definition of food security, and from the food systems literature. This step was taken because my understanding of an explicit reference moves beyond just looking for the term food security and/or food insecurity, as this is too narrow of a focus. Rather, I looked for descriptions of food security and related aspects to food security, which moves into the literature on food systems. The choice of Rocha's (2008) definition amongst other definitions of food security is based on the definition having multiple aspects that make up achieving a state of food security; thereby making it a comprehensive view of the concept. For instance, the aspect of *agency* means that in order to achieve food security, there needs to be policies and processes in place at any level of governance. The onus is on policymakers to act, to put into place assurances that people will be able to meet their food needs (see Lang & Barling, 2012, for further discussion on limits to the term food security). In other words, the effects of the term must trickle down to people in need. The emphasis on *policy* moves away from the emphasis that food insecurity is a result *of a lacking of some sort* within the individual, and/or the individual's failure to attain a state of food security.[3] Moreover, this definition draws attention to food security being achieved through a focus not only on food being culturally acceptable but also on the production of food and how it is obtained (i.e., through food banks).

In term of looking for related aspects of food security, I analyzed the data for instances such as a discussion of seeds, land, soil, natural resources, and biotechnology. Once located within the data, these aspects were highlighted for further analysis. This step was informed by the literature review and the theoretical framework. The relevance of the inclusion of these related aspects is significant because they allowed for a broader analysis of what and how the concept of food security is understood or could be understood when taught by teachers and then interpreted by students.

I understand the occurrence of food insecurity and the achievement of food security to be an interconnected, integrated and an interrelated issue amongst a myriad of aspects, such as the state of the world's natural resources (see Pinstrup-Anderson & Watson, 2011; Rosegrant et al., 2014), the cultivation and security of seeds (Shiva, 2013), and conventional food production practices and the alternatives (e.g., small-scale production) (Gomiero et al., 2011).

I expended some time on this stage and went back and forth with the list against the review of literature to ensure that I had captured a thorough enough coverage of the repeated items from the review of literature to my list. I also paid attention to the terminology used in the curriculum documents against the terminology used on my list when I began the initial data analysis to see if the terminology was close enough to each other. This was done to ensure ease of documentation, and potential conversation points with participants in terms of the items/terms that are utilized in the curriculum documents, and to use the language that could be used across subject matter disciplines as these are the documents that I would be asking about during the interviews. In essence, I was looking for fluency, to not utilize terms that were too lopsided to be based on the language used in food security and food system literature. For me, this was an issue of how to label the section that was being coded for further analysis.

Analyzing the Data: Stage 1

The first round of data analysis was broken up into two smaller parts. The first part was to organize the data into manageable pieces. This step was the coding of the data with the numbered list items, as well as the preliminary coding of the interview transcripts. The second part was reading the data against the literature review to help inform my reading of the data for Stage 2, which is the application of the theory against the data. I have provided these details below organized by data set.

Curriculum Documents and Policy Documents. In terms of the Ontario Ministry of Education curriculum documents, I read the documents, page by page. This included reviewing the Introduction, The Program, and The Considerations for Program Planning in the respective documents. The glossary was also referenced. These aspects were read as part of looking at the overall structure of the curriculum documents, as well as the discussion of the topic and for potential strategies. The policy documents were read in their entirety as well. I reviewed all the documents listed as forms of data mentioned above and scanned for indications of descriptions of the concept of food security (this become a numbered list of items), rather than only looking for the term food security as I mentioned above. As I conducted my search, I noted the prominence of the types of indications of descriptions such as soil or seeds were present, for instance. Completing this step was a way for me to look across the subject matters areas and see what patterns were forming for specific indications of descriptions across various subject matter. I conducted this process by working from the elementary grades to the secondary grades. This part of the data analysis assisted in the building of an understanding of the coverage of the topic of food security in the curriculum documents and policy documents before I moved on to the application of the theory. This step resulted in the following documents and sections within the documents being included for further analysis. In the elementary curriculum documents, the following subjects were included: (1) health and physical education, (2) science, and (3) social studies. In the secondary curriculum documents, the following subjects were included:) Health and physical education, (2) science, (3) technological education, (4) social sciences and humanities, (5) Canadian and World Studies (geography, history, civics (politics) (Grade 9 and 10), and (6) Canadian and World Studies (economics, geography, history, law, and politics) (Grades 9 to 12).

Other policy documents that were included are the following: *Environmental Education Scope and Sequence of Expectations (the elementary level is 2017a and the secondary level is 2017b)* for both the elementary and secondary level, *Shaping our Schools, Shaping our Future: Environmental Education in Ontario Schools (2007b), Acting Today, Shaping Tomorrow (2009c),* and *School Food and Beverage Policy: Resource Guide (2010a), and Health Canada Eating Well with Canada's Food Guide (2011).*

These documents were excluded for further review:

Native Studies, Grades 9–10, 11–12, and

Interdisciplinary Studies, Grades 11–12

The exclusion of these documents is because I was not able to locate any indications of descriptions of the topic of food security and food related aspects.

Program Overviews and Course Descriptions. The documents analyzed within these data sets were the program overviews and course descriptions for the faculties of education in which the participants worked. The same process of reading the texts and selecting portions of texts that illustrated evidence of content on food was completed, as well as applying the numbered list item.

In addition, I noted whether the courses were mandatory or optional in the respected teacher education program analyzed. This allowed me to gather insight as to the potential possibilities for whether a teacher candidate would be exposed to the course or not.

Interviews and Syllabi. Once the transcriptions were completed, I conducted the same steps I had with the documents, I read the transcriptions and applied a numbered list item to the appropriate sections in the transcripts. This step flagged the specific aspect of food security the participants referred to in their interviews (through discussing their ideas and understandings of the concepts of food security and related food items), such as the aspect of food deserts. Also, this step allowed for me to see what specific aspect of food security was covered within the integration strategies discussed by the participants.

After this stage I read the transcripts again and coded sections of the text that reflected the intentions of the interview which was to get an understanding of how participants define the concept of food security, and to learn about what participants are doing to integrate the topic of food security, how are they doing this integration, and if there are challenges to integration. These aspects formed the basis with which I read the transcripts. I then proceeded to refine these initial codes into more clustered codes, by grouping together types of strategies of integration, for instance. This led to the development of themes and allowed me to see patterns across the interview data. Some of the themes and patterns had commonalities with aspects of integration as well as alignment with definitions and related food aspects outlined in the review of the literature.

In terms of the analysis of the syllabi, the same steps were applied as above (application of numbered lists), reading the syllabi for the types of readings, activities, and definitions of food security. Additionally, the syllabi were read prior to the interview, and this allowed me to cross check the activities outlined in the syllabi with the intentions of the design described in the interviews.

Analyzing the Data: Stage 2

The second stage and the last of the data analysis process is the application of the theoretical framework against the data to answer my research questions. My research questions aimed at examining the following aspects: (1) Integration practices across select teacher education programs, and (2) Perspectives (root metaphors) that underpinned the integration practices. I systematically analyzed the data for different aspects of EcoJustice Education. The aspects I applied to the data are the following: (1) The 6 points of EcoJustice which includes aspects such as the commons, a global/local dynamic of understanding issues related to Ecojustice, and curricular development and pedagogical strategies such as cultural ecological analysis and community-based learning, (2) Concepts which pertain to understanding an issue such as relationships, connections, multidimensional, equitable, inclusivity (social), and social and ecological justice (as these concepts are part of the larger concept of EcoJustice); and (3) The perspectives (root metaphors) of both Sustainable Cultures and Western Modern Cultures.

To answer my first research question, I specifically looked for different aspects of EcoJustice Education that spoke to integration practices across all the data which are numbered above as 1 and 2. For instance, I read the data for occurrences of community-based learning practices and cultural ecological analysis with the influence of language on the practice of participants. Part of this step also involved the application of the definition of EcoJustice Education against the data to further provide the types of recognition points that are illustrated through these practices as forms of integration. Moreover, applying the definition of EcoJustice Education allowed me to gain insight into how the data are presenting an EcoJustice version of teaching the topic of food security.

To answer my second research question, I went back over the data and analyzed the highlighted texts for perspectives which refers to number 3 (mentioned above). For instance, as I read the highlighted texts from the curriculum documents, I read the text more closely and analyzed language as in keywords/and or phrases represented in the text around the food-related term against the list of perspectives to see what was being implied by the language used in the selected text. From data gained through the interviews, I analyzed excerpts to see what perspective underpinned the participants' understandings of food security and food related aspects. Also, within this stage, I kept in mind if the data worked towards enhancing an EcoJustice understanding of food security or worked against it through cross-checking the data against the definition of EcoJustice Education. Lastly, I looked across the data moving from the curriculum documents to the interviews (and syllabi) to examine if there were any similarities, differences, and/or linkages.[4]

SUMMARY

My work was designed as a descriptive qualitative study. Two sources of data collection methods used were document review and interviews. The documents collected were from teacher education programs, as well as the official Ontario Ministry of Education curriculum and policy documents. Interviews were conducted with five teacher educators from select teacher education programs in Ontario. I utilized the theoretical framework of EcoJustice Education as a lens with which to interpret the ways in which accounts of integration practices on the integration of the topic of food security in select teacher education programs in Ontario occurred during my investigation.

ENDNOTES

1. The faculties of education chosen for this study in Ontario, Canada are full four-year universities, with teacher education certification programs requiring two years to complete.
2. The focus on urban areas is not to overshadow the fact that food insecurity exists in rural areas. However, this discussion is beyond the scope of this study.
3. See literature on food sovereignty that discuss aspects of the definition of food security.
4. All themes which are shown in the following chapters were pre-chosen and informed by the literature review, and from the theoretical tenets of EcoJustice Education as shown in Stages 1 and 2 of the data analysis procedure. Themes such as "Raising Awareness of Interrelationships" (Martusewicz et al., 2011), for instance, contain a citation to indicate that the theme was informed by the theory whereas in other instances such as "Non-Commodified" (as a perspective in Chapter 6) is a pre-chosen theoretical concept.

CHAPTER 5

INTEGRATION PRACTICES ON THE TOPIC OF FOOD SECURITY IN SELECT TEACHER EDUCATION PROGRAMS IN ONTARIO

The main purpose of this study was to document an account of integration practices of the topic of food security in select teacher education programs in Ontario. In pursuit of this investigation, I sought to explore integration practices at two levels: in practice at the program and classroom level and in perspectives—that is the ways of thinking—which underpin the practices of integration.

There are three main findings in this study that depict integration using document analysis and interviews. I have organized this chapter by first discussing the first two findings, which essentially look at how programs in teacher education integrate the topic of food security and the actions of the participants. The next portion of the findings answers the second research question by illustrating and discussing a deeper understanding of the conceptualizations of food security contained within the documents analyzed, and in the thinking of the participants in relation to the practices that unfolded toward the integration of the topic of food security.

I have also provided the reader with an overview of the main findings whereby I list the subthemes found under each main finding. Moreover, the reader will notice there are a range of different ways of understanding the concept of food security articulated by the participants. Also, the reader will notice that not all the participants commented on each of the integration practices—thereby illustrating that each participant expressed their teaching practices differently. The difference in teaching practices can suggest that there are a range of possibilities for integration to occur on the topic of food security.

OVERVIEW OF MAIN FINDINGS

The analysis of the data revealed the following overarching findings pertaining to both the research questions in relation to the integration practices in select teacher education programs. The overarching aspects of the findings are detailed below:

1. Integration at the program level lacks evidence of a systemic approach in programming, teaching (aspects of integration practices) with subthemes of *course type (i.e., the specific subject-based course), and the status of environmental and sustainability education in selected teacher education programs,* and in curriculum (content) with subthemes at the elementary and secondary level.
2. Integration at the classroom level shows evidence of a systemic approach through strategies such as: (a) community-based learning with subthemes of *raising awareness of place and local issues, raising awareness of how to provide healthy and sustainable schools (communities), and raising awareness of interrelationships* (Martusewicz et al., 2011); (b) evolving toward cultural ecological analysis, (c) developing a global/local outlook (Martusewicz et al., 2011) on food security. Moreover, in this finding, the data illustrated challenges to integration practices, and suggestions put forth by the participants noted under the theme—thinking the way forward for further integration.
3. Integration by way of perspectives suggests a moving toward a systemic approach through the prominence of Sustainable Cultures across all of the data sets. For the data analyzed from the curriculum and policy documents, the perspectives of community-centered, non-commodified, and holistic/organic are shown.
For the data analyzed from interviews with participants and the related documents of the participants, the perspectives showed understanding of the topic of food security held by participants

Educating About/for Food Security Through Environmental Education 71

as being community-centered, and holistic/organic. Lastly, the perspectives which made up the integration practices were holistic/organic and multidimensional, social justice and inclusivity, and (inter) relationship with food and because of food (Martusewicz et al., 2011). In contrast, the data set of the curriculum documents contained perspectives of Western Modern Cultures and are the following: anthropocentrism, progress, and mechanism (application of technology), and science/reductionism.

INTEGRATION AT THE PROGRAM LEVEL

The findings at the program level show an approach to integration that is inconsistent in three aspects: programming, teaching and curriculum (i.e., curricular planning and implementation). The importance of examining whether there is a systemic approach to integration rests on determining if there is any consistency (as in consistent application) to what teacher education programs are doing or offering in terms of opportunities for integration. Consistency here does not refer to the suggestion that teacher education programs must all be enacting integration in the same way. Rather, documenting consistencies in the application of the topic of food security in teacher education programs allows for the data to demonstrate whether there are occurrences of integration, and for the development of an understanding of potentialities toward integration of the topic of food security at the levels indicated (programming, teaching and curriculum).

Programming

The recognition of a lack of a systemic approach through programming is understood to be about whether there is a link between the program overviews of the select teacher education programs in this study, to the instruction level within the same teacher education program. The data indicated that only one teacher education program has direct mention of the topic of food sustainability (related to food security). This objective within the teacher education program of Tulip College (pseudonym) states that as part of the alternative learning placements, students will learn "about local food sustainability and environmental leadership." The other faculties of education included within the data set do not contain a direct mention of food security or food sustainability content in the program. Therefore, as a whole, integration of the topic of food security is non-existent at the program level, so as to act as a form of support (e.g. institutional or policy) for current and future integration.

Teaching (Aspects of Integration Practices)

The following elements show the ways in which the topic of food security is being put into practice within selected teacher education programs.

Course Type and Strategy Used for Integration. The data on the type of courses used for integration are illustrated in Table 5.1 under the heading of *course used in integration*. Table 5.1 also shows how the strategy was utilized within the course.

Table 5.1

Title: Course Type and Strategies Used for Integration

Name of institution and participant (Pseudonyms)	Course used in integration	Strategy used to integrate the topic within the course
Maplewood College Martin	Issues in Secondary Education: How to teach for sustainability in the 21st C? (e.g. place-based, food security education)	Professional learning community Community service -learning project
Greenbank University Alexis	Science (Primary/Junior) Environmental Education	Environmental issues through science STSE strand (Science, technology, Society and Environment) Core engagement of the class
Tulip College Stephanie	Alternative placement (open to all students)	Learning garden (garden-based activities)
Seedsboro University Beatrice	Environmental Education across the curriculum	Big ideas socioeconomic and environmental
PanCanadian College Harvey	Global Issues and Education	In process

The data in Table 5.1 indicate an overall patchwork in the type of courses used by participants. A commonality noted is the use of Environmental Education as a course type regarding integration and is shown by two participants Alexis (Greenbank University) and Beatrice (Seedsboro University). A second course type that emerged is an *Issues* based course with Martin's course at Maplewood College, focusing on issues pertinent to secondary education, and Harvey's course (at Pan Canadian College) based on global issues in education. The remaining course types are an alternative placement, which is open to all students that choose this option in their teacher education certification, and through a course on Science (Primary/Junior). The notation of the types of courses used was to glean whether a pattern of integration is developing in teacher education programs as to how the topic of food security is being taught. At this stage of documented integration, there is no consistent pattern aside from the use of EE in the five faculties of education analyzed for this study.

In regard to the strategies used among participants, there is no indication of a pattern forming as to the types of strategies used, as the data indicates a wide range of strategies. This observation, in conjunction with the course type used by participants, suggests integration is also not consistent to allow for the development of strategies (that may work for other participants).

The Status of Environmental Education in Select Teacher Education Programs. These findings are from online program reviews posted for each teacher education program, in which a participant was interviewed for this study. In all five of the teacher education programs, environmental education and/or education for sustainability courses were offered. However, the offerings of the courses varied whether the course was a mandatory requirement of the program, such as at Maplewood College, or an elective at Greenbank University. Moreover, some participants, such as Alexis and Martin chose to integrate environmental and sustainability-related issues (as the connector to food security) in related courses such as Science (Alexis) or Issues in Secondary Education (Martin). Lastly, the example at Tulip College (Stephanie) indicates that the learning garden acts as a source of learning about environmental education and food sustainability as being aspects which are tied together. The finding on the status of EE courses demonstrates the potential opportunities for the incorporation of the topic of food security through EE, regardless if participants are integrating food security in this manner.

Lack of a Systemic (i.e., Cross-Curricular) Approach in Curriculum (Content)

These findings are from a review of the curriculum documents, whereby I searched and analyzed for descriptions of integration of the topic of food security as directly mentioned, as well as food-related aspects in both the elementary and secondary curricula in Ontario.[1] The analysis is demonstrative of a potential content level integration of the topic in teacher education programs. In other words, the analysis of the content contained within the curriculum documents on the topic shows what is or could be integrated within current and future teaching practices. The findings illustrated that content integration is not occurring in a holistic, nor in an interdisciplinary manner. This finding is exhibited through the related aspects of food security mentioned in the elementary grades, and a direct mention of food security and related aspects in the secondary grade level. Moreover, within the categorization of the grade level, there is a subject-based demonstration of where the related aspects of food are contained within the curriculum documents. This finding is not to suggest that the coverage of the topic of food security is haphazard in the documents, or that the teaching of the topic would also be haphazard. Rather, what is being suggested is the need for the topic to be taught from more than one subject area, thereby utilizing a range of curriculum documents.

At the Elementary Level. Direct mention of the definition of food security does not occur in the elementary grades. In addition, related aspects of the topic of food security are present in both the elementary and secondary grade levels, although not necessarily in *concentrated* ways. Again, by related aspects, I am referring to aspects that make up or are part of the understanding of food security. At the elementary level, there are several examples placed throughout the subject areas, such as in *Health and Physical Education* and in *Science*. Content is presented through *Health and Physical Education* with a focus on Making Healthy choices through healthy eating practices in Grade 2. This requires a building of knowledge by having students "use Canada's Food Guide to assess the nutritional value of meals (e.g., in terms of food groups and number and size of servings) and identify food and beverage choices that enhance healthy growth and development" (Ontario Ministry of Education, 2015b, p. 108). The requirement of learning about healthy eating (through nutrition guides) continues throughout the grades. Additionally, as part of healthy eating is the recognition or the ability to make connections for healthy living, as required by Grade 7 students to "demonstrate an understanding of personal and external factors that affect people's food choices and eating routines and identify ways of encouraging healthier eating practices" (Ontario Ministry of Education, 2015b, p. 200). Content on related aspects such as plants are present in the *Science* Grade 3 curriculum. Plants are discussed through the idea of understanding life systems with the example of "describe the different ways in which plants are grown for food (e.g., on farms, in orchards, greenhouses, home gardens), and explain the advantages and disadvantages of locally grown and organically produced food, including environmental benefits" (Ontario Ministry of Education, 2007c, p. 72). The topic of soil is also present in Grade 3 *Science*. The aspect of soil is presented to have students explain the relationship between humans and soil through asking students to "assess the impact of human action on soils, and suggest ways in which humans can affect soils positively and/or lessen [and] prevent harmful effects on soils" (Ontario Ministry of Education, 2007c, p. 80). In Grade 6, there is attention paid to understanding life systems in biodiversity, through the example of:

> Assess the benefits that human societies derive from biodiversity (e.g., thousands of products such as food, clothing, medicine, and building materials come from plants and animals) and the problems that occur when biodiversity is diminished (e.g., monocultures are more vulnerable to pests and diseases). (Ontario Ministry of Education, 2007c, p. 113)

At the Secondary Level. The topic of food security is directly discussed through curricular objectives in the secondary level *Social Studies and Humanities Grades 9–12* document, specifically in the *Family Studies* subject area. Within the Family Studies subject area, the topic of food security is found in the course *Food and Nutrition* presented under the strand Local and Global Foods in grades 9 or 10, with the course type being Open. Content on the topic asks students to "identify the components of food security (e.g. availability, accessibility, adequacy, acceptability, sustainability)" (Ontario Ministry of Education, 2013b, p. 160), or:

> Explain why some people in Canada cannot achieve food security (e.g., lack of access to safe drinking water in smaller communities or communities with deteriorating infrastructure; low income; lack of knowledge about nutrition or food preparation; lack of resources or lack of access to resources; poor growing conditions or low crop yields as a result of soil depletion or natural disasters). (Ontario Ministry of Education, 2013b, p. 160)

Subsequently, the topic is again discussed in Grade 12 through the *Nutrition and Health* course at the University and College course types and are both found in the strand of Local and Global Foods. At the university level, the curricular objectives review the component of food security (e.g. *availability, accessibility, adequacy, acceptability, sustainability*) but with the aspect of explaining the importance of each component (p. 188). As part of learning the content knowledge, students are asked to "evaluate various food-distribution systems in terms of their impact on local and global food security (e.g., systems that improve the availability of fair-trade products and local foods versus imported foods)" (Ontario Ministry of Education, 2013b, p. 188). Part of the content at the college preparation level is similarly stated to the curricular objectives at the university level in regard to a specific point on food security. For instance, students are asked about food distribution systems, that is:

> Explain how various food distribution systems affect food security, locally and globally (e.g., farmers' markets supply local foods from identifiable sources; large supermarkets provide increased access to foods year-round but may contribute to lack of access to foods in other countries; fair-trade networks guarantee the working conditions of the food producers but may lead to choices to grow cash crops rather than food for local consumption). (Ontario Ministry of Education, 2013b, p. 199)

Similarly, to the elementary grade level, examples of related aspects to food security are contained within the secondary grades. For instance, the aspects of food production and supply are described in the strand Local and Global issues within the subject of *Social Studies and Humanities* at both the university and college level. At the college level the aspect asks students to "outline how geographical factors, physical conditions, and natural disasters (e.g., climate, weather, soil conditions, proximity to water, mudslides, floods, earthquakes) affect supply and production" (Ontario Ministry of Education, 2013b, p. 199). Another example of food production and the environment has students:

> Explain how consumer food choices affect the environment, locally and globally (e.g. demand for imported food increases the amount of energy used in transportation; choice of overpackaged products increases the volume of waste going to landfills; demands for fair trade products supports sustainable farming practices and small-scale farmers but many cause farmers to grow cash crops, such as cocoa and coffee, rather than food; demand for local produce supports farmers' markets, reduces the use of preservatives, and lower transportation costs). (Ontario Ministry of Education, 2013b, p. 189)

This specific food-related aspect is also seen in the *Canadian and World Studies* curriculum (in the subject of Geography, strand Liveable Communities), at the Grade 9 academic level, whereby students are to "analyse the effects of food production practices, distribution methods, and consumer choices on the sustainability of Canada's food system" (Ontario Ministry of Education, 2013c, p. 84). In addition, the issue of natural resources is cited as an aspect requiring attention by students, through instances whereby students "identify the main natural resources that are harvested/ extracted in the region (e.g., water, wood, oil and/or gas, coal, minerals, fish, cotton, wheat, rice, livestock)," and "assess the sustainability of current rates of harvesting/extraction" (p. 138), and by which natural resources are understood to affect "the relationship between the availability and use of different kinds of natural resources and the changing needs of human populations" (Ontario Ministry of Education, 2013c, p. 238). A focus on the commons is illustrated by "explain[ing] the meaning and geographic significance of the commons (i.e., common-pool resources such as water, fish, fishing grounds, forests, common pastures) and the global commons (i.e., the atmosphere, the oceans, outer space, and Antarctica)" (p. 203), and through the requirement of:

> Analyse issues related to human impacts on the global commons (e.g., threats to ocean life as a result of increased shipping, overfishing, and acidification; increased air pollution and climate change as a result of industrial activity)[and to the] international management of the commons (e.g., lack of international authority to regulate the use of the global commons; difficulty of getting countries to subordinate national interests to the welfare of the planet. (Ontario Ministry of Education, 2013c, p. 271)

Health-related aspects of food are contained within the *Health and Physical Education* curriculum. A Grade 9 curricular objective adds to the continued aspect of building knowledge of the effects of social and environmental factors to healthy eating by having students:

> Analyse the influence of social and environmental factors on food and beverage choices (e.g., financial status, culture, religion, media influence, peer influence, family food traditions, accessibility of different kinds of food, restaurant choices, proximity to where food was produced, environmental impact of food production methods). (Ontario Ministry of Education, 2015c, p. 106)

Additionally, the health-related content of food is taken up in *Health and Physical Education* curriculum through learning about nutrition principles. For instance, Grade 9 students are to:

> Apply their knowledge of basic nutrition principles and healthy eating practices (e.g., relating food intake to activity level, ensuring their diet includes foods from all food groups in Canada's Food Guide, using healthy preparation methods) to develop a healthy eating plan. (Ontario Ministry of Education, 2015c, p. 104)

Understanding healthy eating also asks students to:

> Assess the food requirements and available food choices of people in a variety of life situations (e.g., the elderly, children, people with chronic diseases, women who are pregnant, families with low income, residents of remote northern communities, urban residents living in "food deserts" without ready access to fresh and local foods, shift workers, workers in sedentary occupations, individuals training to be elite athletes), and [for students to be able to] describe the options available to them for maintaining a healthy diet. (Ontario Ministry of Education, 2015c, p. 158)

There is also the discussion of health-related content on nutritional principles, as shown in the *Health and Physical Education* curriculum in the *Technological Education* curriculum. The curricular objectives are written with comparable content. For instance, knowledge acquisition on health is to:

> Identify the essential principles of nutrition as referenced in Canada's Food Guide and accompanying resources (e.g., Eating Well with Canada's Food Guide [2007]; Eating Well with Canada's Food Guide: First Nations, Inuit and Métis; cultural adaptations of Canada's Food Guide available from the Ontario Public Health Association). (Ontario Ministry of Education, 2009b, p. 250)

Learning about the topic of food security, as in defining and elaborating on its components, are concentrated in the *Social Studies and Humanities* curriculum. The related aspects of food security are discussed in various subjects such as *Health and Physical Education, Canadian and World Studies and Technological Education*. There is also content on the related aspect of food through *Science*. Two examples are mentioned in the Grade 11 to 12 *Science* curriculum, which are biodiversity and biotechnology. The recognition of biodiversity is discussed in terms of understanding its significance as in "explain why biodiversity is important to maintaining viable ecosystems (e.g., biodiversity helps increase resilience to stress and resistance to diseases or invading species)" (Ontario Ministry of Education, 2008b, p. 51). An example with technological applications to biology is illustrated through the aspect of biotechnology by which students need to "evaluate, on the basis of research, some of the effects of genetic research and biotechnology" (Ontario Ministry of Education, 2008b, p. 68).

As evidenced, the content on the topic of food security is mentioned in the secondary level curricula, as well as several related aspects to food security (as outlined in the literature review chapter of this thesis). In the elementary grades, students are exposed to related aspects as well, but not the direct mention of the topic of food security. The concentration of the topic of food security in the secondary level presents a disconnection in knowledge building from the elementary to the secondary level. Moreover, the related aspects of food security that are presented in the elementary grades are largely documented through the *Health and Physical Education* curricula and leaves related aspects of food security to be taught by teachers (either at the level of teacher education) or in the classroom level (elementary and secondary).

At both the elementary and secondary levels, there is an absence in the inclusion of the topic of food security and First Nations' People in Canada. Specifically, the lack of information is within the realm of building understanding about the causes and effects of food insecurity within Indigenous communities as well as how food and food security are understood not only as concepts but experienced by Indigenous populations.

In sum, the first finding shows a lack of evidence of systemic integration of the topic of food security, as the data were read across and throughout the select teacher education programs investigated. To clarify, there is no pattern of cohesiveness in application across teacher education programs when the data are analyzed to present a picture or snapshot of how integration is happening in select teacher education programs across Ontario. Even as the data are analyzed within each teacher education programs, there are inconsistencies in application such as in programming (at the program level to instruction), in the teaching aspects of course type and status of EE, and in the content of the topic across the elementary to secondary grade levels, and within subjects areas of the curriculum documents.

INTEGRATION STRATEGIES AT THE CLASSROOM LEVEL

In this section, the findings demonstrate integration strategies of teacher educators that are reflective of an EcoJustice orientation toward integrating the topic of food security in their respective practices in three ways: community-based learning, cultural ecological analysis and developing a global/local outlook. Notably, throughout the integration strategies, there is evidence of a connection between the intention of the teacher educator and the design of the integration activity, which I indicate under the overarching integration practice. Also noted within the integration strategies is the occurrence of challenges experienced by teacher educators.

Community-Based Learning: Connections to School and the Community

Three of the participants used strategies and activities that sought to connect students to the community and the places in which they live to learn about food-related issues. From this standpoint, I observed that the participants using community-based learning were—in addition, trying to build another layer of understanding in tandem with learning about food (more broadly) and food security. This aspect of their integration strategies is reflected in three understandings: raising awareness of place and local issues, raising awareness of how to provide healthy and sustainable schools (communities) and raising awareness of interrelationships.

Raising Awareness of Place and Local Issues. Through an environmental education course, Alexis created the opportunity for teacher candidates to experience connections to the places in which they live through a community inquiry action project. As outlined in the course syllabus, the intention of the project is "aimed at developing a learning experience for students in the outdoors and/or environment" with a theme or issue of the community inquiry action project having an "environmental or ecological focus" as well as a "local or global context." There were teacher candidates in her class who worked directly with a local community organization, as in a community garden organization.

In this strategy teacher candidates learn from the ground up, in the sense that they develop an understanding of the issue through inquiry-based practice of researching and working with the organization to understand how the organization deals with the issue. The teacher candidates could coalesce the learned understanding into a product that links back to curricular expectations. To assist her students, Alexis also suggested several resources from the Ontario Ministry of Education, such as *Shaping our Schools, Shaping our Future: Environmental Education in Ontario's Schools (2007b)*, and *Acting Today, Shaping Tomorrow: A Policy Framework for Environmental Education in Ontario Schools (2009c)*. Moreover, she provided resources that focus on place such as Sobel's (2004) *Place-Based Education*, and Gruenewald's (2003) article, the *Best of both Worlds: A Critical Pedagogy of Place*.

The intention in the design of this strategy is based on Alexis's belief of having a contextualized view of food through place as a way for students to be "grounded in our local realities", and for "making things authentic for our students, both culturally, physically, socially, and emotionally." The fact that Alexis aims to make an explicit connection between place and food indicates that she considers a place to be inseparable in learning about food.

In regard to the community service-learning project, as Martin described it illustrates a similar view of providing teacher candidates with the opportunity to link local issues with food. Moreover, Martin focused on having teacher candidates "think about the local community agencies" that are doing work in their communities to address issues as in the lack of access to food. By working with food programs in Toronto, such as Foodshare, Martin stated this group "does a lot with schools," learning about food through their different programs can "make the curriculum more real in the everyday." The service-learning project also contained (as Martin stated) an element of volunteering with these food programs that moved beyond providing a space to observe "just you know the community coming together having food" to a space to examine the "experiences of other people." For instance, he considers the service-learning project to act as a situation that draws the students to be "alert" to how staff and students are experiencing being at the food program. Martin felt the use of this strategy allowed for observation of whether the food programs formed another kind of "charity model" or a place to look at and understand the connection between the socio-economic challenges that "lead to that, to a lack of access" to food. This strategy suggests an alignment with the participant's desire to construct an activity that allowed teacher candidates to be aware of broader issues occurring in the community in which the students live.

Raising Awareness of how to Provide Healthy and Sustainable Schools (Communities) (Martusewicz et al., 2011). Another strategy Martin used to foster understanding about the role of food in our daily lives as well as the lives of the school community is by an activity based on a professional learning community workshop. As described in Martin's course syllabus, "school communities (educators, staff, students, parents, and community members) encounter numerous persistent and pressing issues. The responses to these issues are shaped by Ministry and board policies; professional and personal experience; and consideration of examples of "best practices" (even research!). Moreover, as the course activity sheet outlines the workshop-based activity is constructed with the intention of teacher candidates working with each other "to investigate, assess and recommend policies and programs designed to address persistent, pressing issues," such as "how to provide healthy and sustainable schools for all?" Since the activity is based on teacher candidates investigating policies and programs, students become familiar with several resources which are located on the Ministry of Education of Ontario website, which are *Supporting Minds: Promoting Students' Mental Health & Well-Being (2013d); Open Minds, Healthy Minds (2011) Healthy Schools Initiatives (2013e) (including a focus on Healthy Food) and Environmental & Sustainability Education (including Greening Schools/Eco-Schools*, 2010c). Within this list, many teacher candidates work with food provision programs, and according to Martin, these "food programs are being connected to another part of the assignment" which is an initiative in schools. The initiative links to high school specialist majors whereby high school students are given the space to connect with culinary arts, green food technology, and with a couple of high schools working with small scale agriculture. The food grown through these activities is part of the catering activity that the high school students run out of their high school. The teacher candidates see first-hand what issues and potentialities as teachers they may address, in conjunction with seeing "that the issue of food connect[s] to curriculum, connect[s] to community, connect[s] to employment opportunities, and connect[s] to these policy initiatives to try to make teaching hands on." Martin, through the construction and implementation of this activity evidently views the use of professional learning communities as a conduit to show teacher candidates how schools play a vital role in promoting healthy eating, and the types of foods that are served in schools as part of food provisioning.

Raising Awareness of Interrelationships (Martusewicz et al., 2011). Through an alternative placement of a learning garden, the teacher education program to which Stephanie belongs provides teacher candidates with opportunities to learn about local food sustainability, as well as related concepts of eco-literacy and environmental leadership. As outlined in the learning garden certificate brochure, "teacher candidates will learn through planning and garden-based pedagogies that have a school-community link." Teacher candidates, as the brochure states, "will be engaged in environmental education connections to the Ontario curriculum through language arts, math, science and social studies, physical and health education, and the arts." Through this mandate of the learning garden teacher candidates will be assisted in learning how to implement the *Acting Today, Shaping Tomorrow: Environmental Education in Ontario Schools Policy Framework (2009c)* across the curriculum.

The purpose of the learning garden, as Stephanie reinforced, is to serve as a space to not only build the skills and knowledge required of teacher candidates, but raise awareness of interrelationships. Stephanie is referring to the interrelationships that exist between all things. Building this understanding is assisted through having Indigenous elders discuss "traditional teachings around these kinds of things." Traditional teachings "allow you to think about these things differently." This kind of teaching, Stephanie emphasized, is something "many [students] have never had," so "then working with experts who understand these kinds of interrelationships who have been trained in these ways to get you to move into a school." To supplement the teacher candidates' learning of traditional teachings, and of learning gardens, Stephanie provides a list on the program brochure of several references such as Gregory Cajete's (1994) *Look to the Mountain: An Ecology of Indigenous Education* and Dilafruz Williams and Jonathan Brown's (2002) *Learning Gardens & Sustainability Education: Bringing Life to Schools and Schools to Life.* The learning garden is considered by Stephanie as being "a school but it is a learning garden school outdoor community space." This sentiment is further shown through her words of "you know for the love of the land bringing the children out there to be in place, in the landscape" to have the experience of "a nourishing place." Teacher candidates, through this alternative placement, learn how to teach children about food in an experiential way and not about "learning about food in a book ... in an abstract order." These opportunities, Stephanie feels, foster a connection of the "growing of food and having relationships with place and ecosystems." The use of this strategy for Stephanie suggests that understanding food sustainability and the teaching of food sustainability needs multiple perspectives.

Developing a Global/Local Outlook of Food Security (Martusewicz et al., 2011)

Through classroom-based activities, two participants explicitly created opportunities for students to learn about the global/local connections with the topic of food security. Both participants, Alexis and Beatrice, through their instructions, asked teacher candidates to consider and compare their locality in relation to food security while also considering the environment. For instance, Alexis utilized photos of two separate families living in two distinct geographic locations around the world. The students are to analyze the photos for comparisons regarding how much food per week is consumed, and what types of food (fresh or processed and/or packaged) are in the photos. During the activity, Alexis stressed to the students that "these are real families from all around the world, [and] they don't represent every family from that country, but a sample."[2] This strategy, according to the participant, is useful in pushing teacher candidates to consider one's food situation juxtaposed with another's, thereby allowing teacher candidates the opportunity to make personal connections. Moreover, the activity acted as an entry point to discuss environmental ramifications of packaging in relation to food, also in relation to the teacher candidate's own lives.

The second participant, Beatrice, through placing the topic of food production/security as a Big Idea as outlined in her course syllabus for Environmental Education, provided similar guidance to her student. Beatrice recounted what she told her student about the activity. The student was to create an activity that teacher candidates could use once they begin their teaching careers at the high school level. Beatrice's advice to the student was grounded in having the student "think about for whom food is insecure." Her intention was to convey the message of understanding the global/local dynamic in terms of the concept of food security. Beatrice emphasized by developing thinking that is based on "at least begin [ning] to understand what is happening globally, we want to begin to understand locally." The use of this strategy to elicit a global/local outlook for food, may imply for the participant that to understand the problem, teacher candidates need to be given the space to see the connections, so that a bigger picture of the issue can be formed.

Evolving Toward Cultural Ecological Analysis

Two participants, Alexis and Stephanie, used strategies to teach the students in their respective courses about the influence of language and knowledge systems in regard to understanding food. Alexis and one of her colleagues created an activity in which students had the opportunity to reflect upon the classification of food items (e.g., carrots, parsnip, a rose, a red pepper) and the history of the classification of these food items. Some of these food items, according to Alexis, were "obvious," and by that she meant "our local culture connected to it, so like an apple versus a persimmon." At the onset and throughout the activity, the names of the food items were not told to the students. All the food items have relative relationships with each other. The classroom discussion centered on the history of classification of how these different foods are related from a scientific perspective, and as she stated "how there could be multiple ways of classifying these various things, like you could do it by colour, by shape, you could do it by medical property, you do it by growth season, harvest season, and by the shape of the leaves." The point Alexis was trying to convey through her words is "that there are all sorts of ways that modern western scientific knowledge is privileged over other ways of knowing." Part of the activity, as Alexis articulated by using food items, was to unpack how this came to be, and to highlight what she believed are important aspects such as "issues of cultural appropriation, ways of knowing, oppression of knowledge, and the value of scientific classification." The teacher candidates through this activity were encouraged to question their own established understandings of these food items.

Stephanie had a similar strategy through part of the workshop in the learning garden alternative placement. Through the workshop, teacher candidates engaged in conversation, first from a historical understanding of the ideas of food and food sustainability to what individuals today may understand and think about food and its sustainability. After this step, the teacher candidates with the guidance of Stephanie learned about the educational theory of EcoJustice in that they discussed the linkages between, as she explained "language and knowledge systems," and how language influences the way individuals come to know what they know—and in this case as Stephanie stated, "about food, soil and something growing."[3] Moreover, Stephanie hopes teacher candidates as a result of this new learning will "have something different in mind" for what it means for food to be sustainable, and to translate this learning into their future practices as classroom teachers.

By way of these strategies, both participants sought to assist teacher candidates in moving along a different way of thinking and engaging with food. This engagement with food and the concepts of food security and food sustainability involves a critical lens, that is an understanding toward a not for granted approach to engaging with the planet. In constructing these two activities, it could be understood that deconstructing what one already knows is as important as how this knowledge is constructed in the first place.

CHALLENGES TO INTEGRATION PRACTICES

These findings are based on interviews with participants and illustrate challenges that are varied in nature. In other words, in this study, teacher educators all experienced different types of challenges, meaning that all the participants did not experience the same challenge. However, the challenges experienced by the participants fall under two main categories: conceptualization of the topic, and implementation of the topic in practice.

The first challenge noted in the findings is based on the conceptualization of the topic of food security. To clarify, how the topic of food security is understood can affect how it is taught and how it is addressed in and through education. For instance, Martin stated that he is aware that there may be others [teacher educators] integrating the topic, but others [teacher educators] are not "sharing the practice so as to make it sufficiently impactful" and that could be based on how "food security has been conceptualized in a way as being more core to thinking about the role of being a teacher in the way schools operate." Martin continued the conversation about this challenge by stating that he also believed that the value of food or the role that food is understood to play can be an infringement upon integration. The example he gave is that food can be seen and understood as a sort of "something that is provided as snack program" or as an enticer to get "kids to attend meetings," or as Martin believes "food is a core kind of understanding to building inclusive classroom practice."

Related to this understanding, Martin raised the idea that food, and in particular food choice is not seen as an "intimate demonstration of the connection between food, the environment and sustainability." For some, Martin felt "sustainability is about education around saving lights, turning off the lights, and recycling." Rather, food choice, as Martin conceptualized, "is an expression of our priorities around how we engage with our planet."

Stephanie also raised the same concern, in that if food is taught in an abstract manner (through books) rather than experienced (through the learning garden), the development and continuation of one way of thinking is maintained. The abstract thinking to which Stephanie referred to is based on the idea of schooling being an "inside endeavour ... where it is really a one world view kind of thinking about schools." These examples suggest that integration of the topic of food security is dependent on how it is recognized (that is conceptualized) by teacher educators regarding their integration of the topic and for future teachers.

The second type of challenge encountered by participants is around implementation of the topic. In this challenge there are several issues toward implementation such as rigidity in the college of teachers, resources on the topic of food security, training (implementation of the topic of food security), and teacher commitment (i.e., the commitment of the associate teachers). Additionally, there is a challenge noted by the researcher in terms of a sense of hesitancy in participation by the participants. These challenges are elaborated upon below.

Martin discussed the issue of rigidity in the college of teachers and in a fixed teacher education program. The rigidity rests on how credits were allotted to field experiences, as part of the requirements for certification. In the past, Martin described that teacher candidates had more opportunities in which they were able "to draw connections between schools and community agencies" by doing internships in places like "FoodShare and other food focused agencies like the Stop," as well as "a number of other kinds of food banking kinds of organizations" which allowed for teacher candidates to learn first-hand about food issues.

Additional issues toward implementation mentioned by participants are aspects such as resources on the topic, training (on integration of the topic), and teacher (associate) commitment in teacher candidate placements. Two participants, Martin and Harvey, mentioned that training and a lack of familiarity with the issues, led to a lack of integration of the topic into practice. Moreover, both the participants stated that resources, or more specifically, "finding suitable resources" could also serve as impediments to integration. Lastly, Stephanie mentioned that once teacher candidates get into schools to complete the required placements, commitment on the part of the associate teachers within those placements affects the implementation of knowledge and skills teacher candidates learned through their teacher training, thereby fostering a disconnection between the theoretical from the practical side of classroom-based integration.

Another challenge toward integration of the topic of food security in select teacher education programs was noted by the researcher during the data collection process, rather than from interviews with the participants. From the onset of the recruitment process, there appeared to be a sense of hesitancy and/or uncertainty about participating in conversations about the integration of this topic in the participants' respective teaching practices. This observation was made because of an extensive recruitment process through which I emailed potential participants. Reponses from the participants illustrated hesitancy or an insecurity about going forward through comments such as "I do a little on food," or "I am thinking about it," and/or "I don't integrate food security in that way," and then closing off the one-to-one email correspondence between myself and the participant. These responses illustrate that the topic of food, and not necessarily food security, is percolating as a topic of interest and concern to the teacher educators that responded. However, for the participants who responded in kind, they remain at this time, and at this stage of development regarding the integration of the topic of food security in their respective practices.

THINKING THE WAY FORWARD FOR FUTURE INTEGRATION

Factors Influencing Integration

Participants were asked whether they felt the organizational focus of the faculty in which they worked influenced their integration practices on the topic of food security. Organizational focus in this context refers to what the faculty aims to have developed or influenced in teacher education programs. For instance, there are programs that have a social justice/equity focus as an overarching framework to teaching. Four out of the five participants explicitly stated organizational foci such as equity and social justice, and environmental and sustainability education and/or a combination of both as evidence in the program overviews of the faculties. From interviews with the participants, it was gleaned that the organizational focus is not a direct influence for integration. There is support felt by the participants from colleagues because of the atmosphere in the faculty. For instance, Martin states he "felt very well supported when making decisions" and "found [himself] situated, working with colleagues who, and very much pursue that kind of orientation." By orientation, Martin is referring to his faculty of education's specific framework around social justice and equity. Stephanie also stated she feels her work and the programs she runs are supported by colleagues and administration. She, too, like Martin, works in a university where there is an environmental focus and is a place where there is "a lot of social justice work" being done.

In terms of integrating the topic of food security, Beatrice mentioned she may be "one of the few in the faculty of education" who would address the topic. She believes autonomy played a role in designing the course as to what is included or not. Beatrice noted that there is not a strong environmental focus at her university, although there are "strong sensibilities around social justice." These findings suggest three points of interest in terms of integration. First, integration is strongly based on what the participants wanted to convey about the topic of food (more broadly) and food security with the design and carrying out of the course. Second, it appears that organizational and institutional support from the faculties in which the participants work does not hinder or necessarily encourage integration, but is present as an overarching framework for the faculties. Lastly, the presence of a social justice framework in conjunction with an environmental focus brings the organizational framework of the faculties toward an EcoJustice framing of integration.

Suggestions for Future Integration

At the closing of the interviews, the participants revealed some thoughts on how to integrate the topic of food security into future practices. One participant, Martin, provided a suggestion for a course to be developed on food issues within schools as a space to coalesce learning about food and how food and schools intersect. In addition, he strongly felt that all students should experience field trips that take them to an abbatoir (a slaughterhouse), to a dump, and to a water treatment facility. The basis for his suggestions is because these are all examples "of things that are hidden from us, as we move through our daily consumption." Therefore, these aspects of our daily consumption, as he stated, "would be good things for our students to learn about in schools." Evidently, learning about these issues in schools ties back to Martin's strongly held belief in the role of school as a place to learn and understood the importance of food and food security (more broadly).

Another participant, Beatrice discussed the point of starting integration of the topic of food in the elementary grades because "you want these ideas to emerge as early as they are doing social studies [for instance]." She continued by saying that learning about food is "not to be in a negative way, but more in terms of understanding food." This is to occur, Beatrice suggested by adapting "that early curriculum throughout the grades and topic areas," so by the time students reach the higher grades, there is a foundation upon which to draw some knowledge and understanding. Similarly, Alexis stated she believes that food is a "great entry point" for elementary teacher candidates, and anyone who is "hesitant or uncomfortable with issues of environmental sustainability or social inequality" to make changes that have far-reaching effects through teaching. Alexis, it seems, is referring here to the inherent cross-curricular nature of examining food issues. Lastly, Stephanie strongly articulated her belief that the topic of food security needs to be thought of in a holistic manner, and the topic should be taught with an integrated model. She said that "we need an integrated model because it is not just one way of thinking [about food security], you need multiple knowledge systems [to address the issue], [and] to think about these complex questions" that are being considered in education. These suggestions from the teacher educators imply that there is a desire to continue to move forward with integration in ways that can push teacher candidates and teacher education to consider the topic of food and food security in a broad manner.

To reiterate, the strategies used within select teacher education programs reflected community-based learning, cultural ecological analysis, and developing a global/local outlook on the topic of food security. This section also discussed challenges experienced by the teacher educators, as well as ideas from the teacher educators as to how future integration could take place. In the next section, the data addresses the second research question, which sought to document the perspectives underpinning integration.

ENDNOTES

1. The findings illustrate that all the participants (except for one) do not directly use the curriculum documents in their teaching practice. By this, I am referring to referencing specific curricular objectives during the activities and/or strategies utilized. The exception is in Alexis's activity. Alexis referenced the Grade 6 science curriculum document with attention to the topic of biodiversity for the classification activity used to teach other ways of knowing (and understanding) when it comes to the classification of food.
2. The photos Alexis used are from Peter Menzel and Faith D'Aluisio (2007).
3. Resources listed for EcoJustice Education are the following: (1) Bowers (2001a, 2006), and (2) Martusewicz et al. (2011).

CHAPTER 6

INTEGRATION BY WAY OF PERSPECTIVES ON THE TOPIC OF FOOD SECURITY

This chapter outlines the perspectives shown through the integration practices within the select teacher education programs for this study. These findings answer my second research question. The presentation of this finding is organized by aspects of integration that I sought to understand such as: (1) What perspectives on the topic of food security are reflected in the documents used in teacher education, (2) What perspectives underpin the conceptualization of the topic held by the teacher educators interviewed, and (3) What perspectives underpinned the integration strategies used in the practice of teacher educators. The results indicate the prominence of perspectives reflective of Sustainable Cultures across all the data sets, whereas the perspectives reflective of Western Modern Cultures are only present in the data set of the curriculum documents. The examples listed below represent perspectives that are contained within the subject matter areas of *Science, Health and Physical Education, Social Studies and Humanities, Canadian and World Studies and Technological Education.*

This section begins with the illustration of the prominence of Sustainable Cultures as noted in the documents and in the interviews. Following this, I outline the examples of perspectives based on Western Modern Cultures found in the data from the curriculum documents.

Educating About/for Food Security Through Environmental Education: An Account of Integration Practices in Teacher Education Programs Across Ontario, Canada, pp. 91–112
Copyright © 2025 by Information Age Publishing
www.infoagepub.com
All rights of reproduction in any form reserved.

SUSTAINABLE CULTURES PERSPECTIVES ON UNDERSTANDING THE TOPIC OF FOOD SECURITY THROUGH INTEGRATION PRACTICES

In this section, I note several instances of the presence of perspectives that belong to Sustainable Cultures. These perspectives were found in all the data and are presented first on the curriculum and policy documents, followed by the interviews with participants and the related documents of the participants. Before proceeding to the detailed analysis of curricular excerpts, I provide the reader with Table 6.1 which briefly outlines the types of perspectives found in the curriculum and policy documents, and with examples of keywords and phrases. The reader will notice there are three main types of perspectives belonging to those of Sustainable Cultures outlined below.

Table 6.1

Title: Examples of Perspectives of Sustainable Cultures Found in Curriculum snd Policy Documents

Perspective	Curricular Excerpt
Community-centered: sees community as a basic social unit. Elders conserve and pass on traditions that sustain community and ecology. Community includes the rest of nature.	"identify local programs to increase food security" (Ontario Ministry of Education [Social Studies and Humanities], 2013b, p. 160). "buying locally, bartering or exchanging, and/or growing their own vegetables" (Ontario Ministry of Education [Social Studies, and Humanities], 2013b, p. 209)
Non-commodified: traditions are maintained based on intrinsic value and meaning. Markets and monetary transactions are a small part of culture.	"cultural variations in daily eating patterns (Ontario Ministry of Education [Social Studies and Humanities], 2013b, p. 157). "childhood eating habits can influence lifelong eating patterns" (Ontario Ministry of Education [Social Studies and Humanities], 2013b, p. 157).
Holistic/organic: see the world as interconnected like a living thing. Views humans and the rest of nature in reciprocal relationship of interdependence.	"interdependence between the living and non-living things" (Ontario Ministry of Education, [Science], 2007c, p. 81). "how various factors affect the availability of local foods" (Ontario Ministry of Education [Social Studies and Humanities], 2013b, p. 159).

Community-Centered. The community-centered perspective rests on the notion that the community is viewed as the basic social unit and includes the rest of nature. This way of thinking in relation to food security and/or food insecurity means that solutions are derived from or centered in and around the community (Ackerman-Leist, 2013). The concept of local in this context is seen as part of the community context. Local as a concept in dealing with food security and/or food insecurity is shown as an example of a community-centered focus towards providing assistance in regard to increasing food security. An example of this is seen through the curricular objective that asks students to "identify local programs to increase food security (e.g., education programs, food banks, community kitchens, community gardens)" and assess their effectiveness" (Ontario Ministry of Education [Social Studies and Humanities], 2013b, p. 160). The language of "local programs to increase food security" (p. 160) suggests that focusing on the community (e.g. community kitchens and/or food banks) plays some role towards addressing the issue (even if the effectiveness of the programs is questioned).

The concept of local can be understood to be seen as a more environmentally friendly way of growing food. For instance, the statement "describe environmentally responsible ways of acquiring food" is reinforced with examples such as "buying locally, bartering or exchanging, and/or growing their own vegetables" (Ontario Ministry of Education [Social Studies, and Humanities], 2013b, p. 209). Moreover, there is a teacher prompt which suggests that "buying locally grown produce help[s] the environment?" (p. 209). In another instance when trying to assess the effects of personal and family food-purchasing and food-preparation practices on the environment, local foods are positioned as food that "require [s] less fossil fuel for transportation" (Ontario Ministry of Education [Social Studies and Humanities], 2013b, p. 159).

Non-Commodified. Food-related activities and the opportunity of food practices related to traditions are viewed as enacting non-commodified ways of engaging with food. A curricular description explaining "why specific foods are served on various special occasions in Canada and in different countries (e.g., national holidays, cultural and religious celebrations, weddings, harvest celebrations, family celebrations)" (Ontario Ministry of Education [Social Studies and Humanities], 2013b, p. 166) exhibits a way of thinking about food in relation to serving as more than an instrumental and functional transaction. Like the example above based on specific food servings as part of one's culture, the effect of "how childhood eating habits can influence lifelong eating patterns" (Ontario Ministry of Education [Social Studies and Humanities], 2013b, p. 157) also illustrates a way of understanding interactions with food to be shaped by personal and social interactions (that are not necessarily money or market centered).

Furthermore, the effect of culture upon food practices is shown through the curricular example of having students build understanding around "cultural variations in daily eating patterns (e.g., time of day for meals, number of meals per day, timing and typical content of the main meal of the day)" (Ontario Ministry of Education [Social Studies and Humanities], 2013b, p. 167). The timing of when or how many meals could imply that there is a traditional aspect attached to food practices.

Holistic/Organic. A holistic/organic view of the world sees the world as interconnected. The interconnections are reflective of a living thing. Part of this way of thinking views humans and the rest of nature as interdependent. The application of holistic/organic thinking towards the topic of food security is demonstrated through descriptions that present the topic as being affected and/or composed of many factors. The policy document *Shaping Our Schools, Shaping Our Future: Environmental Education in Ontario Schools* (Ontario Ministry of Education, 2007b) clearly demonstrates a call toward providing students with "the knowledge, skills, perspectives, and practices they need to be environmentally responsible citizens" (p. 4). As part of becoming environmentally responsible citizens students are provided the space to develop understanding about "our fundamental connections to each other, and to the world around us through our relationship to food, water, energy, air, and land, and our interaction with all living things" (p. 4). The topic of food is shown here as part of an intricate and interconnected engagement of various elements on the planet, and between humans and all living things. This notion is further exemplified by asking students to "describe characteristics of a healthy environment, including clean air and water and nutritious food, and explain why it is important for all living things to have a healthy environment" (Ontario Ministry of Education [Science], 2007c, p. 46).

A particular element of the Earth—soil is seen as having a vital role in supporting living organisms. For instance, soil is made of various components, and "the components of various soils enable the soil to provide shelter/homes and/or nutrients for different kinds of living things (e.g., microscopic bacteria and micro-organisms feed on decaying matter in the soil; roots of plants absorb minerals from the soil)" (Ontario Ministry of Education [Science], 2007c, p. 81). This example illustrates that soil has components within it that serve other living things—the interconnection between the living things in the soil maintains the living things. Moreover, soil is also seen as having "interdependence between the living and non-living things" (Ontario Ministry of Education [Science], 2007c, p. 81). Along a similar line to the role of soil is the aspect of biodiversity. Understanding biodiversity is expressed through learning about "the importance of biodiversity to the sustainability of life within an ecosystem (e.g., variability among biotic and abiotic factors within an ecosystem decreases the chance that any organism within that ecosystem will become extinct)" (Ontario Ministry of Education [Science], 2008b, p. 175). Soil and biodiversity when it comes to understanding food security, can be seen as foundational in that both the aspects of soil and biodiversity serve in providing variations of species upon which food can grow, and the interconnections that occur in the soil and through variations in biodiversity affect not only the quality of food but also the different types of foods, as in crops, for instance (Mohtar, 2016; Shiva, 2005).

The definition of food security is presented as having components such as "availability, accessibility, adequacy, acceptability, [and] sustainability" (Ontario Ministry of Education [Social Studies and Humanities], 2013b, p. 199). The presentation of the topic in this manner suggests a way of thinking about food security as a holistic issue—that is made up of multiple components that could be seen as affecting each other and the state of food security/insecurity.

The same line of thinking is expressed in the following curricular expectation: "evaluate various food-distribution systems in terms of their impact on local and global food security (e.g., systems that improve the availability of fair-trade products and local foods versus imported foods)" (Ontario Ministry of Education [Social Studies, and Humanities], 2013b, p. 188). The understanding that is being generated through this expectation indicates that there are various types of systems that could lead to different kinds of impacts. The issue of the development of knowledge on food security is based on interconnected thinking. Another example on related aspects of food security is "explain how geographical factors, physical conditions, and natural disasters (e.g., climate, weather, soil conditions, proximity to water, mudslides, floods, earthquakes) affect food supply and production and water potability" (Ontario Ministry of Education [Social Studies and Humanities], 2013b, p. 188). This example implies an awareness based on interconnected thinking formed from more than one factor, causing a change in food supply and production.

Examples in relation to food choices describe the same kind of thinking through suggestions of building understanding about "how various factors affect the availability of local foods (e.g., proximity to agricultural land, length of growing season, presence of infrastructure such as greenhouses or fish farms, weather, soil conditions)" (Ontario Ministry of Education [Social Studies and Humanities], 2013b, p. 159) or "how various factors (e.g., geography, religion, economics, culture, environment, values) influence personal food choices" (Ontario Ministry of Education [Social Studies and Humanities], 2013b, p. 175). Also, the instance of "explain[ing] how consumer food choices affect the environment, locally and globally" with examples such as the "demand for fair-trade products supports sustainable farming practices and small-scale farmers, but may cause farmers to grow cash crops, such as cocoa and coffee, rather than food" (Ontario Ministry of Education [Social Studies and Humanities], 2013b, p. 189) illustrates an interpretation of the issue as being connected to another issue. Furthermore, food choices are understood here to be a complex issue as well as interdependent, with interlocking factors such as economics (e.g. pricing of food) connecting with a factor of geography (e.g. location of food), to environmental conditions that span a local to global reach. The combination of factors again makes the issues of food choice (in particular), and food security (more broadly) issues that require a holistic and relational way of perceiving and addressing it.

In terms of building understanding about healthy eating, or about establishing a healthy eating environment, the Ontario Ministry of Education's *School Food and Beverage Policy: Resource Guide* (2010a), suggests an interconnected approach to helping students achieve this goal. The interconnection rests on the entirety of the school environment to teach and reinforce healthy eating by "seek[ing] input from students, staff, parents, and community partners when determining which food and beverages to offer for sale in the school, taking into consideration the diversity of the school population" (p. 54). The same way of understanding the idea that healthy eating is related to food choice is exhibited through several curricular examples which show there are multiple factors that intersect the relationship between food choice(s) and healthy eating. For instance, students are asked to:

> Apply their knowledge of medical, emotional, practical, and societal factors that influence eating habits and food choices (e.g., allergies and sensitivities, likes and dislikes, dental health, food availability, media influences, cultural influences, influence of family and friends, school food and beverage policies, environmental impact, cost) [in order] to develop personal guidelines for healthier eating. (Ontario Ministry of Education [Health and Physical Education], 2015c, p. 173)

Attaining healthy living is also learning to:

> Assess the food requirements and available food choices of people in a variety of life situations (e.g., the elderly, people with chronic disease, women who are pregnant, families with low income, residents of remote northern communities, urban residents living in "food deserts" without ready access to fresh and local foods, shift workers, workers in sedentary occupations, individuals training to be elite athletes), and describe the options available to them for maintaining a healthy diet. (Ontario Ministry of Education [Physical and Health Education], 2015c, p. 158)

Or, that healthy eating is about understanding that students who are also:

Educating About/for Food Security Through Environmental Education   97

> Consumers can have an impact on food and beverage choices at school and in the community (e.g., promoting availability of healthy choices in restaurant and cafeteria menus and in grocery stores, raising awareness of ethical and environmental considerations related to food choices). (Ontario Ministry of Education [Health and Physical Education], 2015c, p. 124)

The ability and opportunities to make healthy food choices need to be understood wherein students can:

> Identify current issues that involve food either directly or indirectly (e.g., issues involving food safety or quality, such as pesticide use, genetic modification of crops, the sale of non-pasteurized milk products; issues involving food marketing and advertising; environmental issues, such as climate change, packaging and waste reduction, water pollution, biodiversity, long-range transportation of food; issues involving agricultural practices, such as humane treatment of animals, labour and trading practices), and [be able to] explain how healthy eating choices are related to these issues. (Ontario Ministry of Education [Health and Physical Education], 2015c, p. 143)

As evidenced, food choices and healthy eating are considered being related, however, their relationship—that is, the ability to make a food choice that leads to healthy eating is shown to require a way of thinking that illustrates these complexities.

There are examples of how individuals and groups of individuals could be affected by interconnected (what could be seen as interconnected) aspects related to the state of food insecurity. For instance, the example of having students "explain how various factors (e.g., genetics, deterioration of infrastructure, environmental governance, trade embargos, war, natural disasters) affect the nutritional status of specific population groups in Canada and around the world" (Ontario Ministry of Education [Social Studies and Humanities], 2013b, p. 185) demonstrate (again) a link in thinking between and among components (listed as examples) which may cause a difference in nutritional status of peoples. Additionally, several other curricular examples describe interconnections of elements at different levels that cause nutritional inequalities such as "assess the role of various factors (e.g., heredity/ genetics, socio-economic status, geography, lifestyle, activity level) in nutrition-related illnesses and health conditions" (Ontario Ministry of Education [Social Studies and Humanities], 2013b, p. 186), or "explain how and why various social, cultural, and economic factors (e.g., gender, ethnicity, income, employment, religious or political affiliation) contribute to nutritional inequalities among people within the same community" (Ontario Ministry of Education [Social Studies and Humanities], 2013b, p. 186), or "describe the relationships between poverty, food insecurity, poor nutrition, and poor health" (Ontario Ministry of Education

[Social Studies and Humanities], 2013b, p. 199). These additional examples also utilize the language of *factors in, and factors contribut[ing] to, as well relationships between*, what affects, and/or causes a state of poor nutrition. Thus, the example can be seen to suggest an interpretation of holistic/organic and relational way of understanding the topic of food security.

Understandings of the Topic of Food Security Held by Participants

Holistic/Organic. One participant described an understanding of the term food security to be an issue that is interconnected to several aspects as well as an issue that is for all people. Alexis stated that she understands food security to be based on the "notion of good healthy, accessible nutritious food for all." Moreover, she considers the term to be "kind of like a blanket term that incorporates the individual rights, responsibility and advocacy all the way up to the broader collective social corporate governance structures." She goes on further to state that the issue is "very complicated, and there are multiple components, [and] stakeholders." Alexis's understanding of the term food security is most closely associated with Rocha's (2008) definition of the 5As approach to understanding the topic of food security. The similarity is based on Alexis's definition containing multiple components, and that the components according to Alexis are grouped together under a blanket term. The grouping together of terms could suggest that the components have equal value toward achieving a state of food security, rather than only focusing on one aspect toward achieving food security.

There is also the understanding among the participants that food security is made up of more than one understanding (i.e., composed of many elements). This was noted through Beatrice's talk when she articulated that the topic of food security is "almost like food understanding like just knowing about your food, so to me there are probably two bits to that right now." The two bits to which she referred to are "[an] understanding of food and then there is understanding of food security." She further considered the topic to be about "a lot of different things," such as questioning "Do we have access to food, [and] can we grow as the climate changes?" as well as reflecting upon the "ethical pieces around food." Although Beatrice did not explicitly state the aspects she outlined are interconnected or are to be seen as such, the language she used indicates that one idea builds upon the other to develop her understanding of food and then food security.

Community-Centered. Understanding the topic of food security to be contextualized within a community (as place) was also observed (although slightly differently) among two participants. Martin, for instance, described his understanding of the topic of food security to be about schools as the sources of learning about food-related issues. Schools, for Martin, are a contextualized place "where there are all sorts of policies around food," as "students will work in schools often where there are food programs." From this statement, Martin wants his students to learn, understand and "draw on their own sensibilities" when it comes to grasping the realities of a lack of access (e.g. food, and/or financial) that may or may not be gained through a discussion of the definition of food security.

Stephanie explained her understanding of food security "to be something taken on at a local level." The local level for Stephanie was described as an understanding that has "to be a generational thing." She also felt that building awareness of food security is around a certain way of thinking:

> There is your local global situation where we need to be able to eat the foods within our local, so if you think about if from the perspective that we live in a particular landscape and then you adapt to that landscape.

She concluded her thought with "you know [we] find ways to think about the commons, and the things that are being enclosed." Thus, Stephanie's statement shows understanding of community-centered perspectives in alignment with an EcoJustice way of relating to the world.

Perspectives Underpinning Participants' Integration Practices. The perspectives shown by the participants all illustrate an alignment with thinking that is reflective of *Sustainable Cultures* perspectives. Furthermore, what is interesting to note is the observation that all the participants, regardless of the distinctions present within the descriptions given, illustrate commonalities and connections among the integration strategies utilized.

These similar aspects illustrate an overview of *interconnected thinking*, in that the strategies utilized by the participants seem to create opportunities for teacher candidates to make connections between one aspect or several aspects related to understanding food security, and/or through one site of learning with another.

Holistic/Organic and Multidimensional (Martusewicz et al., 2011). Beatrice's perspective on integration appears to reflect the same understanding she put forth in her description of the term food security. For Beatrice, the objective was to draw her student's attention to seeing the interconnectedness of the topic of food (and food security more broadly) to the environment, as shown in her course syllabus. Through the course syllabus Beatrice wanted students to build knowledge of food security (listed as a "big issue" on her course outline) in the context of seeing these interconnections of "local and global environmental sustainability effect people in both the local and global context but in different ways." Moreover, her view that "food security is a lot of different things" further underpins the perspective (she displayed through her strategy and defined) as multidimensional.

Social Justice and Inclusivity (Martusewicz et al., 2011). To reiterate, Martin sought to bridge healthy school policy initiatives to larger issues in society by having teacher candidates focus on food programs in schools as well as community service-learning projects. The planning and implementation of this strategy falls under the perspective of a social justice and equity orientation to teacher education, whereby as far as school experiences go, Martin wanted school experiences to "be commented, read, analyzed and interrogated through this lens, and so how it is that schools either respond to those inequities, challenge those inequities or reproduce those inequities." This perspective was enacted through Martin's desire to bring students (teacher candidates) attention past the serving of food in a community center, to attention being drawn toward inclusivity through experience. Martin stated, "I was drawing them to be alert to, so how are staff and students experiencing this, is it an example of where they feel included." Or, as pointed out above in regard to Martin's concern about replicating charity model approaches to understanding and dealing with food security, it is his concern of whether this situation is "somehow experienced as a moment of shame and are they othered through this process." Evidently, Martin's concern is for the building of awareness on the issue of inclusivity or a lack thereof when it comes to people's access to food, as food for Martin is "an exciting opportunity to make real the everyday opportunities for learning."

(Inter)relationship With Food and Because of Food (Martusewicz et al., 2011). Both Stephanie and Alexis illustrate a perspective of relationship when it comes to understanding food. Stephanie's strategy of a learning garden emphasized through the design a relational understanding of the world. Food, and the cultivation of food through the learning garden is "understanding relationships—ecology—it is really about the study of relationships and that has to come into play" when trying to build awareness and knowledge about topics such as food sustainability (the focus of the learning garden) and food security. As the learning garden's structure is shown through the alternative placement brochure, the learning garden is to provide teacher candidates with the opportunities to "experience planning and garden-based activities at a school-community site." The experience for teacher candidates in building knowledge about what food sustainability means will have the relational aspect of seeing the link between the school and the community.

Similarly, Alexis discussed her belief that "food is truly tangible," the tangibility of food for Alexis is explained through the fact that "we put it in our bodies, it is a physical thing outside our body, and then we put it in our bodies, so we have a physical reaction, an emotional reaction." Thus, for Alexis, "we have all kinds of things that are connected to our relations with food." From this statement, it is implied that Alexis sees food as a conduit to understand relationships with food, and with self, and reinforces the strategy of contextualized learning about food.

WESTERN MODERN CULTURES PERSPECTIVES ON UNDERSTANDING THE TOPIC OF FOOD SECURITY THROUGH INTEGRATION PRACTICES

In this section, I note several instances from the curriculum and policy documents that demonstrate the presence of perspectives reflective of Western Modern Cultures. Before proceeding to the detailed analysis of curricular excerpts, I provide the reader with Table 6.2 that briefly outlines the types of perspectives found in the curriculum and policy documents and with examples of keywords and phrases. The reader will notice there are three main types of perspectives belonging to those of Western Modern Cultures outlined below.

Table 6.2

Title: Examples of Perspectives of Western Modern Cultures Found in Curriculum and Policy Documents

Perspective	Curricular Excerpt
Anthropocentrism: sees humans as the center and dominant over the rest of nature. Ignores consequences of human activity. Exhibited in such terms as "natural resources."	"managing natural resources" (Ontario Ministry of Education [Science], 2008b, p. 175). "extracting or harvesting of natural resources" (Ontario Ministry of Education [Science], 2008b, p. 174).
Application of technology: This is a combination of both progress and mechanism. Progress: seen as linear and usually progressive, but irresistible regardless. Exhibited in such terms, "you can't stop progress," and in assumptions that "newer is better," experimenting on nature is good. Mechanism: sees world and life processes as being like a machine, exhibited in such terms as "information processing and "feedback systems."	"artificial selection technology (e.g., livestock and horticultural breeding)" (Ontario Ministry of Education [Science], 2008b, p. 52). "the impacts on food production on resource use and the environment in Canada" (Ontario Ministry of Education [Canadian and World Studies], 2013c, p. 96).

(Table continued on next page)

Table 6.2 (Continued)

Title: Examples of Perspectives of Western Modern Cultures Found in Curriculum and Policy Documents

Perspective	Curricular Excerpt
Science/reductionism: is seen as the most legitimate way of knowing, objective and culture free: separate from morality. Reductionist—analyzes complex phenomena by breaking into parts. Knowledge is only high status if it is derived from rational thought and formal schooling.	"apply[ing] their knowledge of basic nutrition principles" (Ontario Ministry of Education [Health and Physical Education], 2015c, p. 104). "assess the basic nutritional values (e.g., in terms of carbohydrates, proteins, fats, vitamins, minerals)" (Ontario Ministry of Education [Technological Education], 2009b), p. 257).

Anthropocentrism. In regard to understanding the topic of food (broadly) and food security (more specifically) and the aspects that comprise this state, an anthropocentric mindset is evident when discussing *human intervention* (risks and benefits) and biodiversity (of aquatic or terrestrial ecosystems). The curricular objective demonstrates use of language reflective of anthropocentrism through "stocking lakes with fish provides recreation for fishing enthusiasts and increases the amount of food available for humans and other animals" (Ontario Ministry of Education [Science], 2008b, p. 50). Yet, there is also present in the objective the understanding that this may in fact "affect the natural biodiversity of the aquatic ecosystem" (p. 50). Food availability becomes contingent upon humans intervening in the functioning of the food system regardless (perhaps) if risks arise. The process of making food available is like other forms of human intervention toward biodiversity (to produce food) (Sage, 2012).

A similar example is expressed through phrasing such as "the benefits that human societies derive from biodiversity (e.g. thousands of products such as food)" (Ontario Ministry of Education [Science], 2007c, p.113). The benefits again are not without consequence, as this deriving creates "problems that occur when biodiversity is diminished" (p. 113). Within this example, there is the mention of the use of monocultures systems. These systems "on farms allow crops to be grown in the soil that is best for them. But monocultures systems reduce biodiversity, and so more soil and pest problems result" (p.113). The cyclical nature of the benefit and risk through the use of monocultures is further exemplified by the application of "more chemical fertilizer and pesticides, which pollute the land, the water, and the food they are producing" (p.113). Moreover, the cyclical nature could be construed as literally feeding benefits to humans at the expense of the rest of nature.

Educating About/for Food Security Through Environmental Education   103

Viewing nature as a resource for human use is also frequency documented. The language of describing "characteristics and properties that make a natural resource viable for use (e.g., the size, type, and location of trees; the value, location, and extraction and processing costs of minerals)" (Ontario Ministry of Education [Science], 2008b, p. 175) and to "natural resources alongside "harvested/extracted in a [particular] region" (Ontario Ministry of Education [Canadian and World Studies], 2013c, p. 137), whether it be in reference to water, fish, or wheat indicates that this understanding places humans at the center of this exchange when resources are extracted or harvested for human consumption. Asking students to further "assess the sustainability of current rates of harvesting/extraction" (p. 137) or "assess the environmental impact of industrial practices related to the extracting or harvesting of natural resources, and describe ways in which that impact can be monitored and minimized" (Ontario Ministry of Education [Science], 2008b, p. 174), juxtaposed these descriptions, also indicate at some level an awareness of the effects of this human-centered mindset toward nature. Students are further encouraged to "describe programs in the region that are intended to foster stewardship/sustainability with respect to natural resources and to assess their effectiveness" (Ontario Ministry of Education [Canadian and World Studies], 2013c, p. 138), or "describe strategies that industries and governments have implemented to increase the sustainability of Canada's natural resources" (Ontario Ministry of Education [Canadian World Studies], 2013c, p. 78). There is a similarity between these examples in the back and forth thinking that is occurring whereby the action of natural resources extractions are done, and then the consequences to the resources are considered. Furthermore, through the example "explain how overhunting and overfishing as well as the reduction or elimination of natural habitats have affected on the availability of foods found in different regions of Canada" (Ontario Ministry of Education [Social Studies and Humanities], 2013b, p. 168) shows another form of understanding nature as a resource that has gone past a point of balance. Both examples related to the process of an *over* in relation to human interactions with nature are noted ways of sourcing food. Moreover, as stated in the curricular objective, form part of a link that leads to lower levels of food supply connected to food availability, which in turn are connected to states of food security and/or insecurity (Rosegrant et al., 2014).

Another illustration that shows the influence of anthropocentrism when it comes to understanding and thinking about "natural resources" is the idea of the distribution of resources and the effects of this distribution through:

> Analyse relationships between the distribution and availability of natural resources in a country or region and its quality of life, as reflected by

various indicators (e.g., life expectancy, infant mortality, per capita income, average years of schooling). (Ontario Ministry of Education [Canadian and World Studies], 2013c, p. 199)

Additionally, the idea that natural resources need to be managed in order for them to be sustainable or shared equitably is presented. This idea is clearly expressed through the passage of "explain the importance of managing natural resources to ensure sustainability and biodiversity" (Ontario Ministry of Education [Science], 2008b, p. 175). Or through the passage of "describe policies and strategies used in various countries to manage natural resources sustainably" (Ontario Ministry of Education [Canadian and World Studies], 2015a, p. 236).

Through analysis of issues pertaining to and related to "the use and management of shared resources," such as "common-pool resources (e.g., fish, water, the atmosphere …)" (different objective, p. 236), students are asked to question "who owns common natural resources that flow between or across political boundaries?" (p. 236). This question provokes a way of thinking that seemingly could be constructed as in defense of "common-pool of resources" but is lessened by the language of managing and management of shared resources. The same line of thinking is noted with reference to the "human impacts on the global commons." Examples such as "threats to ocean life as a result of increasing shipping, [or] overfishing" (Ontario Ministry of Education [Canadian and World Studies], 2015a, p. 271), along with understanding how these impacts relate to the "international management of the commons" (p. 271). The actions as stated are human driven resulting in an impact which affect not only other humans (as the commons has a cultural and social component) (Shiva, 2005), but other living things and ecosystems, that in turn contribute to the overall supply of food (Vivero-Pol, 2014). As the managing of the global commons is an international issue, the anthropocentric thinking that underpins this example in the first place (arguably) creates a way of thinking applied to sorting out another issue such as a "lack of international authority to regulate the use of the global commons" (Ontario Ministry of Education [Canadian and World Studies], 2015a, pp. 271–272). Or for the issue of the commons to be analyzed "from a legal perspective [in] the strengths and weakness of international laws to protect key natural resources held in common around the world (e.g., water, air, fish)" (Ontario Ministry of Education [Canadian and World Studies], 2015a, p. 490).This way of thinking can perhaps further suggest the inquiry as to whose benefit is the control of resources and/or the commons (global or not), and is this control serving human consumption and potential development or some other objective?

Progress and Mechanism. The progressive way of thinking is demonstrative of considering human actions toward change as a necessary part of reality—a part of reality that contains the understanding that progress is unstoppable. Part of this momentum forward is seeing new as better, and as more needed than the current way in which one engages or interacts with reality. As mentioned above, one way of thinking can feed into another way of thinking, so progressive thinking has as part of it, the idea that humans are dominant over nature (anthropocentrism), thus experimenting on nature is seen as good, and as a way forward. Also tied to the progressive way of thinking is mechanistic thinking. Mechanistic thinking refers to seeing the world and life processes as a machine.

Application of Technology. This type of thinking in food-related activities is evident in agricultural methods and practices and is positioned as a potential solution to food supply and food production problems. Yet embedded within the same language of progressive and mechanistic thinking is the need to literally address problems that could be attributed to the *application of technology* to the same problems. For instance, the phrase "analyze, on the basis of research, the economic and environmental advantages and disadvantages of an artificial selection technology (e.g., livestock and horticultural breeding)" (Ontario Ministry of Education [Science], 2008b, p. 52) exemplifies the idea that technological application does in fact provide positive and advantageous results toward breeding of livestock and horticulture. The sample issue of the above statement is written as "selective breeding of agricultural crops can benefit populations in less-developed countries by producing hardier crops, increasing food supplies, and improving the nutritional content of food" (p. 52). The assumption underpinning the advantageous nature of human intervention toward producing more food is shown in the same sample issue through "opponents of artificial selection technology believe that it affects the natural ability of a species to reproduce, which negatively affects biodiversity" (p. 52).

Another example of the application of technology in relation to food is through the application of biotechnology. Through this example in which there are connections made to "social issues related to an application of biotechnology in the health, agricultural, or environmental sector (e.g. issues related to the uses of genetically modified organisms...)" (Ontario Ministry of Education [Science], 2008b, p. 236). The way in which technological applications are applied to food positions the scenario of biotechnology as beneficial for humans in that it leaves out the effects of this technology. For instance, the sample issue states, "the promise of genetically modified (GM) crops was that they would be resistant to pests and would produce more abundant harvests" (p. 236). Again, like the example above, the progressive way forward toward finding change in terms of how food is produced, created what could be considered as a negative consequence of this type of thinking through realizing that "GM crops can crossbreed with crops in adjoining fields, thus contaminating traditional food sources, reducing biodiversity, changing farming practices, and limiting the choices available to consumers" (p. 236). The language in the sample issue of "the promise of" GM crops despite the noted negative consequences indicates that experimenting on nature will potentially have positive outcomes and create (for some) an irresistible step forward toward justifying the use of technological applications on nature without necessarily not knowing the full consequences.

Understanding the effects of genetic research and biotechnology on the environment (specifically) further raised an issue of awareness that connects to the same type of thinking. Students are asked to "evaluate, on the basis of research, some of the effects of genetic research and biotechnology (e.g., genetically modified organisms [GMOs]) on the environment" (Ontario Ministry of Education [Science], 2008b, p. 68). This curricular objective is qualified with a sample issue of looking at the benefits, and of altering farmed salmon against the potential damage toward wild fish, as in understanding that:

> Farmed salmon can be genetically modified to reach market size in half the time of normal fish, and cost half as much to feed. However, entire populations of wild fish could be endangered by mating with bioengineered fish that are released into the wild, with disastrous consequences for the ecosystem. (p. 68)

The discussion of the benefits and damages toward the environment and nature in regard to technological applications with food, and the connections to food security, are documented. Thus, it is not surprising that tensions are presented within the curriculum.

There are in addition other examples which ask students to understand through analysis the "ethical issues of biotechnology (e.g., with respect to the use of bacterial insecticides, the patenting of modified microorganisms)" given that "genetically modified microorganisms are used in many biotechnological applications that benefit humans, in areas such as food production" (Ontario Ministry of Education [Science], 2008b, p. 66). A follow-up sample question posed is a discussion of "Should suppliers be required to label foods that have been modified using microorganisms, so that consumers can make more informed decisions about the food they eat? Why or why not?" (p. 66). Another example adds to the discussion of the ethical implications of biotechnology by asking students to "analyze the social and legal implications by citing instances such as the bioengineering of animal species, especially those intended for human consumption; the cultivation of transgenic crops; the patenting of life forms [and] cloning)" (Ontario Ministry of Education (Science), 2008b, p. 82). A sample issue used to qualify this curricular objective is the fact that:

> Corporations that have patented genetically modified (GM) seeds legally require farmers to buy new seeds from them each planting season. Corporations that find GM crops on a farm that did not purchase their seed can take the farmer to court. However, natural processes such as cross-pollination can result in the migration of GM crops to neighbouring farms. (p. 82)

The way of thinking embedded in these examples follows the idea of going forward in trying to resolve issues, such as a lack of food supply through technological applications without full consideration of the consequences. This lack of consideration leads to discussions of many implications that have resulted from the choices made in the first place.

The progressive view as it applies to aspects of food and food security is noted in relation to *food production*. For instance, the statement of "the impacts on food production on resource use and the environment in Canada" (Ontario Ministry of Education [Canadian and World Studies], 2013c, p. 96), can indicate that food is produced in a machine-like manner, and because of this type of engagement with food, there are direct impacts on resources and the amount of resources available to grow food for future use (at this pace of production).

The effects of this mentality are further shown in the following curricular excerpt, whereby students are to "analyse the effects of food production practices, distribution methods, and consumer choices on the sustainability of Canada's food systems" (Ontario Ministry of Education, (Canadian World Studies), 2013c, p. 84). There are built-in tensions within this objective through the way food is produced and creates notable effects upon the long-term (or not) of Canada's food systems.

Another curricular example exhibits the same thinking of the application of technology by stating that there are effects "on the environment" by having students analyze the effect of "various agricultural trends (e.g., growing crops for biofuels) and food production technologies (e.g., types of farm equipment, types of energy sources, climate-control techniques, genetic engineering of foods)" (Ontario Ministry of Education [Social Studies and Humanities], 2013b, p. 189). Thus, the understanding put forward by phrases such as food production technologies can imply that the use of technology to create food can cause a chain of cause and effect, which is built into this process of adding food to overall food availability.

In another instance, technological advances such as "irradiation of food, development of genetically modified foods, use of growth hormones in livestock, use of flavour enhancers [and] increase in convenience products"

(Ontario Ministry of Education [Technology Education], 2009a, p. 267) emphasize *changes* that "have affected food production and consumer spending" (p. 267). An illustration of technological advances with the element of advantages and disadvantages is also shown through the following passage "analyse the social and economic costs and benefits of the use of non-nutrient food additives in food preservation and food enhancement techniques (e.g., sulfites in dried fruit; food colouring; MSG)" (Ontario Ministry of Education [Science], 2008b, p. 232). The passage through the sample issue further demonstrates two sides of technological advances in that "non-nutrient food additives increase the shelf life of many foods, and decreas[es] waste from spoiled food [which] allow[s] foods to be transported around the globe" (p. 232). By being able to transport food globally, consumers are given an increase in food choice, while at the same time "it also increases carbon emissions and can hurt the Canadian farm economy" (p. 232). The passages suggest that the technological applications toward foods are experimental and have in fact affected the actual creating of food, and how consumers themselves spend on food products. The impetus toward using technology to solve a problem can at times, skew the consequences created by the changes such as in potential health consequences.

In line with changes toward food supply and food production in relation to the environment, there is a concern for the "effects of various environmental protection laws and regulations on food supply and production (e.g., policies related to forest preservation, fuel emission standards, pesticide use)" (Ontario Ministry of Education [Social Studies and Humanities], 2013b, p. 189). The concern can be seen as tensions in thinking in regard to making changes to food, and then having to institute protection and regulation laws because of the need to increase and continue with (the current) food production practices. This way of thinking is further shown through a curricular objective which puts forth integration of the topic by asking students to "demonstrate an understanding of health, safety, and environmental issues related to food supply and production" (Ontario Ministry of Education [Social Studies and Humanities], 2013b, p. 189). The example presented for this objective discusses the "risks [then] associated with the bioaccumulation of pesticides and hormones, [and] risks of contamination during food production)" (p. 189) along with "key aspects of legislation that is designed to protect Canadian consumers (e.g., Canadian Agricultural Products Act, Food and Drugs Act) (p. 189). In essence, the progressive and mechanistic thinking that pushed food production practices in a certain direction has subsequently led to legislation designed to protect the Canadian consumer from the effects.

Science/Reductionism. When it comes to attaining a state of food security in regard to one's health, there are several instances that illustrate

Educating About/for Food Security Through Environmental Education

a scientific and/or reductionist perspective. A scientific and/or reductionist way of thinking analyzes and presents complex phenomena by breaking it down into parts. However, breaking down the concept of health and the attainment of health and nutritious food into parts (of understanding) on a path toward achieving food security can leave out related factors that cause food insecurity. The majority of examples throughout the curriculum and policy documents that contain knowledge about healthy eating illustrate similar examples of understanding healthy eating to be about building knowledge in terms of learning about nutrition principles and/or standards. For instance, the Ontario Ministry of Education policy document *School Food and Beverage Policy Resource Guide* (Ontario Ministry of Education, 2010a), presents nutrition standards to "embody the principles of healthy eating outlined in Canada's Food Guide" (p. 7), and illustrate "nutrition criteria that apply to all food and beverages offered for sale on school premises for school purposes" (p. 7). Understanding nutrition in this context is about meeting the implementation of standards that could be interpreted as reducing the achievement of nutrition and healthy eating to having these standards met in schools. The same line of thinking is exhibited through curricular objectives across various subject areas. For example, learning about healthy eating is based on the ability to:

> Identify the essential principles of nutrition in Canada's Food Guide and accompanying resources (e.g. Eating Well with Canada's Food Guide [2007]; Eating Well with Canada's Food Guide; First Nations, Inuit Métis; cultural adaptations of Canada's Food Guide available from the Ontario Public Health Association). (Ontario Ministry of Education [Technological Education], 2009b, p. 250)

In addition to identifying essential nutrition principles, understanding healthy eating is about students:

> Apply[ing] their knowledge of basic nutrition principles and healthy eating practices relating food intake to activity level, ensuring their diet includes foods from all food groups in Canada's Food Guide, using healthy preparation methods) to develop a healthy eating plan. (Ontario Ministry of Education [Health and Physical Education], 2015c, p. 104)

Another example asks students to:

> Assess the basic nutritional values (e.g., in terms of carbohydrates, proteins, fats, vitamins, minerals) of a variety of food products, using appropriate resources (e.g., Eating Well with Canada's Food Guide [2007]; Eating Well with Canada's Food Guide: First Nations, Inuit and Métis). (Ontario Ministry of Education [Technological Education], 2009b, p. 257)

Or a combination of both "identify[ing] the sources and explain[ing] the functions of macronutrients (i.e. carbohydrates, fats, proteins), micronutrients (i.e. vitamins, minerals), and water" (Ontario Ministry of Education [Social Studies], 2013b, p. 184).

Students learn about the use of food groups in making food choices through "describe how the food groups in Canada's food guide can be used to make healthy food choices" (Ontario Ministry of Education [Health and Physical Education], 2015b, p. 93). Understanding food and healthy eating practices are about the ability to "describe appropriate serving sizes defined in Canada's Food Guide," and "elements of a healthy diet, and [to] demonstrate the practical knowledge and skills required to prepare healthy meals and snacks (e.g., ability to plan varied, nutritious, and economical meals and snacks" (Ontario Ministry of Education [Social Studies and Humanities], 2013b, p. 110). Also, the opportunity to:

> Evaluate personal food choices on the basis of a variety of criteria,
> including serving size, nutrient content, energy value, and ingredients
> (e.g., fats, carbohydrates, protein, vitamins and minerals, calories,
> additives, allergens), preparation, method, and other factors that can affect
> health and well-being. (Ontario Ministry of Education [Health and Physical
> Education], 2015b, p. 217)

The curricular objectives use similar language to the policy documents that healthy food choices are about having knowledge that is scientifically based.

Moreover, the language used in describing healthy eating when read through a lens of understanding food security could suggest the importance of understanding health in relation to food security to be about understanding the components of specific nutrients. Although the recommendations through these curricular objectives for students to build knowledge around nutrient intake is important, what is absent from these examples is the connection of how one's state of health is linked to a person being considered food secure or insecure.

The findings in this section illustrate contrasting perspectives of both Sustainable and Western Modern Cultures as forms of interpretation on the topic of food security. The results show variance in how food-related aspects are discussed within the data through how the language used in describing the perspectives is embedded within the aspects. Tables 6.3 and 6.4 show the perspectives found within all the data for this section of the findings. Table 6.3 is based on the data analyzed from the curriculum and policy documents (although presented separately in this section) shown here side by side to demonstrate the contrast between the documents.

Table 6.3

Title: Comparisons of Perspectives Found in Curriculum and Policy Documents

Perspectives: Sustainable Cultures	Perspectives: Western Modern Cultures
• Community-centered • Non-commodified • Holistic/organic	• Anthropocentrism • Progress and mechanism • Application of technology • Science and Reductionism

Table 6.4 illustrates perspectives of Sustainable Cultures present in the data sets, to show what perspectives are illustrated within the different aspects of the interviews, and the related documents of the participants.

Table 6.4

Title: Perspectives of Sustainable Cultures in All of the Data Sets

Interviews (data on perspectives underpinning participants' integration practices)	Related documents (Syllabi) of the participants
• Holistic/organic and multidimensional • Social justice and inclusivity • (inter)relationship with food and because of food	• Holistic/organic and multidimensional • (Inter)relationship with food and because of food

Tables 6.3 and 6.4 illustrate the variance contained within the data sets which clearly demonstrate a presence of Western Modern Cultures in the curriculum documents, and not in data obtained by the participants through interviews and their related documents. The interviews and related documents exhibit similar perspectives across all four of the data sets, thereby showing similar ways of understanding food security and food-related aspects among the documents and the participants.

SUMMARY

In this chapter, I used the theoretical framework of EcoJustice Education as well as aspects of a definition of integration from the literature review to analyze integration practices on the topic of food security in select teacher education programs in Ontario. More specifically, integration in this sense refers to how the topic of food security is being taken up through teaching practices by teacher educators in the respective teacher education programs in which the teacher educators belong.

Through the analysis of interviews with teacher educators, and document reviews I showed a picture of a systemic approach to integration on the topic of food security across select teacher education programs in Ontario. This result resembles a fragmented presentation, as the occurrences of integration within the teacher education programs analyzed exemplify information that is not coordinated. In other words, there are pieces of integration that vary within and across the faculties of education included in this study. This first finding contrasts with the second finding, where the integration strategies of the teacher educators documented in this chapter show a link between the strategy used and the intention of the teacher educator.

Also noted from the data are challenges in integration practices as experienced by the teacher educators across the different faculties of education, which illustrated a development of the types of challenges toward integrating the topic of food security. The teacher educators as well, were forthcoming in ideas for future integration of the topic, emphasizing the importance of continuing to move forward along this type of educational initiative.

Through the analysis presented in the last finding of this study, I provided examples of two conflicting perspectives that appeared within the data, those demonstrative of Sustainable Cultures and Western Modern Cultures. This analysis revealed a prominence of ways of thinking that align with and promote understanding of food security reflective of Sustainable Cultures. Ways of thinking reflective of Sustainable Cultures are based on ideas of learning and teaching that promote ways of seeing the world as interconnected. That is, when individuals understand the notion that humans are connected to non-humans, individuals' actions have consequences, and that all living things matter and have value, we collectively can move forward toward living sustainably. In contrast to this idea of interconnectedness, thinking associated with Western Modern Cultures is seeing the world as disconnected. Living entities, for instance, are seen and treated as separate from other living and non-living entities, and that individuals' action may or may not be understood to have consequences. The perspectives reflective of Western Modern Cultures were noticeable in the curriculum and policy documents.

CHAPTER 7

CONCLUSION

What to Do About Integration?

SUMMARY

Informed by research on integration practices of food, and EE in teacher education programs, as well as by the theoretical framing used for this, I sought to discover what is happening in teacher education programs around the integration of the topic of food security at the program and classroom level. I was interested in the types of strategies being utilized by teacher educators, such as community-based learning, cultural ecological analysis, and developing a global/local outlook. The reason for this focus rests in how these types of strategies advance a call for understanding the context within which food security as a concept is being enacted. The strategy of cultural ecological analysis pushes for an understanding of food security that is neither just a social issue nor an environmental issue. Rather, the issue of food security/insecurity is multidimensional, and that these dimensions can intersect and feed off each other to compound the issue. Having students understand a global/local outlook on the topic of food security pushes students to see the linkages between actions in one part of the world to another, and to understand others. In understanding one's situation in comparison to another's, students can learn and become

---

Educating About/for Food Security Through Environmental Education: An Account of Integration Practices in Teacher Education Programs Across Ontario, Canada, pp. 113–132
Copyright © 2025 by Information Age Publishing
www.infoagepub.com
All rights of reproduction in any form reserved.

aware of current situations, as well as develop an understanding of why things are the way they are—in terms of states of food security and insecurity around the world.

In addition, I sought to go deeper into understanding in what ways is the topic of food security represented in and through select teacher education programs. For instance, what understandings make up the conceptualizations of the topic of food security held by teacher educators, and what understandings influenced the teaching practices of teacher educators. To accomplish this aim, I analyzed the data for perspectives—utilizing the established perspectives of Sustainable Cultures and Western Modern Cultures (from the theory of EcoJustice Education) as interpretative frameworks of understanding as I read across the data.

The data analyzed suggests integration practices that work for and against the type of integration practices encouraged by scholars in the field of EE such as Evans et al. (2017), and scholars utilizing an EcoJustice framework for education such as Young and Stanley (2018), and Martusewicz et al. (2011). The approach I am suggesting is informed by both the theory and literature review for integration to occur which presents opportunities for learning that are systemic (i.e., coordinated across) within a teacher education program. This means that curricular instruction is encouraged to be cross-curricular in nature, as well as the use of pedagogical strategies that foster spaces for students to see the linkages between their thoughts and behaviors.

In the following section, I outline my interpretation of the significance of the findings toward the overall aim of this study. This is done under each of the findings, which are the following: (1) Integration at the program level lacks evidence of a systemic approach; (2) Integration strategies at the classroom level show evidence of a systemic approach, and (3) Integration by way of perspectives illustrates a moving toward a systemic approach.

INTERPRETING THE FINDINGS

Integration at the Program Level

An overview of the integration practices of the topic of food security in select teacher education programs in Ontario lacks evidence of a systemic approach. The first finding is significant, as this leads to a non-holistic view of the topic. The results mirror a patchwork presentation of how integration is taking place, and in essence show inconsistency in the process of integration. Only one teacher education program had a specific mandate to teach the related topic of food sustainability, and within the same program, there was one participant who taught this topic. Therefore, there is no interconnection shown between programming and instruction that could strengthen integration. Moreover, it could be said that, based on the results, one cannot fully determine if programming is a factor or not toward integration. But, as evidenced in the related literature on the integration of EE, a lack of cohesiveness or implementation of the topic at the administrative level acted as a constraint toward integration (Babiuk et al., 2010; Liu, 2009; McKeown & Hopkins, 2002). Therefore, there is not necessarily an "all hands-on board" approach to integrating the topic in teacher education.

At the teaching level, the results of this study indicate that there is a lack of consistency in the disciplines in which the topic of food security is being taught, aside from EE being cited by two participants. As a result, observing the development of a common course and/or subject matter for future integration by teacher educators is still uncertain. Although there is common ground forming with the use of EE as a place for future integration on the topic of food security in teacher education courses. This may prove difficult given the overall lack of pre-service programs with specific concentrations on EE as noted in the research on EE integration in teacher education programs (Beckford, 2008; Hanchet, 2010; Swayze et al., 2012; Lin, 2002). Nevertheless, the integration that is happening is demonstrative of noted approaches (in the literature review) as in the topic of food security being integrated as an aspect of a core/compulsory subject (Martin's work as a teacher educator is an example). Another example is the use of a learning garden (Stephanie) that is embedded in the alternative placement within the teacher education program in which she belongs. The alternative placement is like a systemic approach to embedding sustainability education across curriculum areas, courses and institutions of higher education (as outlined in the literature review) as the alternative placement is built into the teacher education program, thereby making it a clear option for teacher candidates to choose as part of their experience. Moreover, the alternative placement, as recounted by Stephanie, provides the space for teacher candidates to learn how to integrate the topic of food sustainability into all curriculum areas and their future education practices.

In regard to the curricular level of integration, direct mention of the topic is at the secondary level. As a result, learning about the topic in elementary grades is through related aspects of food security. The teaching of these related topics, such as soil, may (depending on the level of knowledge of the educator) require further connections to be made. In addition, the concentrations of the topic of food security in certain subjects increase the opportunities that the topic may be missed—meaning not all teacher candidates nor teacher educators have or will have the opportunity to refer to the topic when teaching subject-based courses. This uncertainty, according to Liu (2009) is due perhaps to a lack of teacher training and professional knowledge of the topic.

If the topic is contained in concentrations in certain subjects such as *Health and Physical Education* and reflects very specific aspects of food as in nutrition principles, the teaching of the topic in this manner can create silos of information. The "silo-ing" of information works against creating a holistic and interdisciplinary view of the issue (Falkenburg & Babiuk, 2014, p. 423). Rather what is being called for by scholars in both EE (Liu, 2009; Powers, 2004; & Yavetz et al., 2009) and in the field of food security (Allen, 2013) is the bringing together of various subjects to reflect real world connections, because doing so creates the opportunity to realize the multitude of factors that intersect, which ultimately affect the conditions of environmental sustainability and food security.

Another aspect missing within the curricular conversation of food in/security is the connection to First Nations communities within Canada. The discussion in relation to First Nations communities is twofold: 1. There is an absence in the mention of the state of food insecurity experienced by Indigenous communities, and 2. The contribution of First Nations philosophies and ways of thinking on the topic of food and food security. The absence of the dire conditions experienced by Indigenous people in regard to the levels of food insecurity is highly problematic. Indigenous people, as stated in the literature review, experience one of the high rates of food insecurity, particularly in Northern Canada. This gap prevents a sharing of fundamental knowledge about the complexity of the issue within Canada and does not move collective action forward toward ensuring all peoples' rights to food are being understood or met.

The absence of including Indigenous ways of knowing and understanding on the topic of food security through EE further compounds the issue of working toward a solution that includes all voices affected by the issue. The lack of inclusion of Indigenous voices in EE, and Indigenous contributions to create solutions to the very issues that severely impact Indigenous communities, could be seen as favoring Western worldviews. Historically, Western worldviews in relation to the environment further create a distancing of people from the land which moves away from a reciprocal relationship with land (Gorlewski & Porfilio, 2012). This way of thinking is counter to enacting an Ecojustice framework that moves all voices forwards to create a food secure world.

INTEGRATION STRATEGIES AT THE CLASSROOM LEVEL

With this finding, the strategies used by the participants illustrate commonalities while being part of a larger picture of a less than systemic approach to integration in the select teacher education program analyzed for this study. From this observation, it could be understood that integration of the topic is driven by the teacher educator. Specifically, integration is driven by the intention of the teacher educator regarding what aspect of food security was to be conveyed through the course design. For these participants, whether there is an overarching framework for integration, or a mention of the topic in the program overview (aside from one program mentioned) does not affect the integration practices. These actions by the teacher educators could reflect similarity to teacher educators enacting EE by their own commitment, not the commitments necessarily of the program (Babiuk et al., 2010).

The commonality in the types of strategies utilized demonstrates the formation of a set of approaches toward integration, as well as the observation that the development of strategies aligns with the theory of EcoJustice Education. The overarching pattern present in the results of integration shows the idea of building an understanding of why things are the way they are. There are connections to other studies such as Andrée's (2007) work which engages (undergraduate) students with food issues at the community level by pushing students to think about and question the status quo[1]—this push for students to think about, and question the status quo is like Martin's strategy within this study. Moreover, Martin's strategy encompassed a focus on nutrition and healthy eating, which is similar to Elsden-Clifton and Futter-Puati's (2015) work—although these authors take on the interconnection between food, nutrition and sustainability. A study by Harris and Barter (2015) mirrors aspects like Alexis' desire to use place-based approaches to create learning spaces that foster connections to the places in which one lives, to the issue of food security, and to the myriad of factors that intersect between the two aspects. A point of contrast rests in the location of the work, as Alexis's focus is centered in urban centres, and Harris and Barter's focus is on rural areas. Thus, this study is adding to a consideration of using place-based pedagogies as a form of engagement when building understandings of food issues in teacher education classrooms. Lastly, Stephanie's use of a learning garden illustrates a way of making interconnections not only amongst subject areas to teach the related topic of food sustainability, but also amongst and between community members and teacher candidates. The use of a learning garden is seen to increase knowledge on food-related issues, such as food security and sustainability (Williams & Brown, 2012).

In terms of how participants defined the concept of food security, it appeared that participants understand the idea of food security as both "complex and multifactorial" (Godrich et al., 2017, p. 1), which in general aligns with the broader literature on food security and food systems (see the Literature Review chapter of this study). The issue of the concept of food security being considered complex, and in need of multiple viewpoints to understand how to address the issue aligns with the idea of participants not having a standard definition in mind, or the actual use of a standard definition (nor should the participants have to use a standard definition). For the participants, it appears their definitions are broad in scope and are contextualized to their understanding. For instance, one participant described the term food security to be a blanket term, which incorporates a range of broader social issues like corporate governance structures and individual rights. At the core of the participant's (Alexis) understanding of food security, she defined the concept to be "good, healthy, [and] accessible food for all." The fact that not all participants use the definition of food security as defined in the literature, or develop their own definition perhaps is a result of the various aspects which range from personal viewpoints to individual academic backgrounds and teaching preferences of the participants. Moreover, what this finding suggests and reiterates when it comes to understanding issues such as food security, is the notion that there are different ways of knowing that come into effect, and subsequently could affect integration.

The strategies outlined above and within the findings chapters illustrate the connections between the participants' intention and design, and reflect practices informed by EcoJustice Education. The strategies also reflect part of the definition of EcoJustice Education. For instance, Martin's strategy provides the space for teacher candidates to critique and pay attention to socioeconomic factors that cause an imbalance in states of food security or insecurity experienced by people. Beatrice's goal of having teacher candidates understand the vulnerabilities experienced by different people around the world indeed mirrors the recognition of patterns of domination and marginalization of people. Lastly, Stephanie's use of a learning garden provided a space of opportunity for the recognition of intergenerational practices and exchanges of learning about the interconnections of gardening and food sustainability through the incorporation of knowledge held by Indigenous Elders and community members.

As part of the strategies used by participants, it did not appear that curriculum documents played a direct role toward integration. Rather, I noted that participants reflected an indirect use of the curriculum and policy documents leading to what I state as an influencer instead of serving as a director of instruction. I state influencer rather than director as the participants reflected the spirit of the documents. Moreover, as shown above, the participants' action were influenced by their intentions to convey a particular message through their integration practices.

This is not to negate the significance or status of curriculum documents when it comes to learning about the content contained within the documents. A concrete reasoning or significance of this finding cannot necessarily be placed upon the lack of content within certain subject areas on the topic of food security, or upon the lack of knowledge on the teacher educator's part as to where the content is, such as in *Social Studies and Humanities* through a direct reference. By direct reference, I am explicitly stating that reference is made to the topic of food security and food production. Whereas in other subject areas, the onus is on the teacher educator to make connections to specific content (e.g., GMOs) to food security more broadly.

A point of interest in this finding is to consider whether the indirect links in the curriculum are problematic for learning and understanding the topic of food security. The indirect links can provide learning experiences that are random and not systemic. Additionally, the lack of space and opportunity for teacher candidates to learn about the conceptualizations of food security lead even further to a loss of making a direct link to the topic. These observations correspond to Babiuk et al.'s (2010) findings on teacher candidates' learning about sustainability in teacher education. Thus, until curriculum documents become more robust in their articulation of the topic of food security, perhaps teacher education needs to encourage resourcefulness of teacher candidates and teacher educators, which in turn could level out issues of self-efficacy cited as a challenge to the integration of sustainability in teacher education programs (Liu, 2009).

In observing the challenges described by participants in this study, there are several types of challenges, which in turn reflect a lack of consistency. For instance, a challenge noted in the findings as discussed by both Martin and Stephanie is around the conceptualizations of the topic. This type of challenge is similarly mentioned in the EE literature, whereby according to Ferreira et al. (2009), there are few studies that explore teacher educators' perceptions of sustainability. Also, if there is a lack of awareness of a topic such as sustainability, and the relevance of understanding why having an awareness of sustainability is important in teacher preparation at both the faculty and administrative level, challenges toward integration can occur (Babiuk et al., 2010; Liu, 2009; McKeown & Hopkins, 2002). Lastly, the variance in the types of challenges makes it difficult to develop a set of remedies, solutions, or strategies to move the field of study forward for future integration.

INTEGRATION BY WAY OF PERSPECTIVES

The findings indicate a prominence of perspectives—that is a way of thinking about an aspect of reality—to belong to those of Sustainable Cultures across all the data. More specifically, the data shows the prominence of perspectives of Sustainable Cultures in the curriculum and policy documents, the participants' definitions of food security as well as within the participant's integration practices. The illustration reinforces a general movement toward an EcoJustice informed practice of integration in teacher education programs as evidenced above through the consistency of integration practices.

There is consistency in the findings that illustrate an alignment between the participants' definitions of food security, and the perspectives underpinning their integration practices. This finding shows that the definition—considered in this study to reflect understanding and thinking on the issue is playing out through integration practices which reflect the same overarching thinking. The recognition of this dynamic is advocated by the theory of EcoJustice Education, in that how a person thinks about an issue affects the person's actions (Martusewicz et al., 2011), thereby illustrating an EcoJustice informed integration of food security in the teacher educators' practices. The fact that the participants demonstrate thinking that is in alignment with Sustainable Cultures suggests a pushing forward toward creating future integration practices that are seen to contrast with Western Modern Cultures (which are noted in the curriculum documents). However, it is interesting to observe that the participants in their integration strategies did not use (as a whole) the curriculum documents directly. At this point, making a claim as to what is in fact the direct influencer of integration—the participants, or the curriculum, or both is not possible. The relevance of having some evidence about a direct influencer of integration practices, such as the curriculum documents, for instance, could lead to a call for changing the language used in the documents. Furthermore, in the interim of shifting curricula, if there is continued effort to unpack thinking, this in turn could break the repetition in thinking which leads to behaviors that are deemed detrimental to the environment and to attaining a state of food security.

The remaining part of this finding is the concentration of perspectives of Western Modern Cultures found in the curriculum documents. The presence of these types of metaphors are found in various subjects in my analysis—and not contained in only one subject. For example, the presence of anthropocentric ways of thinking are noted in the subject of *Science*. This finding is not surprising, as science has been associated with containing anthropocentric views of the world (Hoeg & Barrett, 2016). Similarly, the subject of *Health and Physical Education* reflected a reductionist perspective, which is noted to relate to a scientific understanding of health, whereby learning about food (its components) is about learning the bits and pieces rather than a larger picture of the role between food security and health. For instance, understanding micronutrients is significant, but there are factors that affect access to foods considered to be required to obtain well-being. Therefore, how education (broadly) and teacher education specifically teach about food can reinforce and promote a way of thinking and learning about health that is potentially prescriptive or medicalized in nature. This is problematic, as these modes of thinking can eventually be passed on to classroom-based practices (Welch et al., 2012).

The presence of Western Modern Cultures in the curriculum documents is concerning, as the curriculum documents do play a role in teacher instruction. Whether or not teacher educators and future teacher candidates consider the curriculum to be the standard of content integration or only a guideline (as in a reference), these ways of thinking are still contained in the documents. In other words, the language used in the curriculum documents reflects something, a value, for instance (Schiro, 2008). As a result of these ways of thinking being contained within the documents, the possibility of teaching them is present. These types of thinking are seen to be detrimental to continuous food security, and toward a sustainable food system (Fullbrook, 2010; Shiva, 1993, 2013). Having these ways of thinking in relation to the concept of food security, if left unquestioned, has the potential to be repeated and passed on through continuous instruction. In regard to teaching and learning of the topic of food security in such a manner further exemplifies the significant role that teacher education can play in continuing or discontinuing ways of thinking that adversely affect the planet (Martusewicz et al., 2011).

An additional observation I made during the analysis of the perspectives within the curriculum documents is the absence of understanding the origins of some of the language used in the text analyzed. For instance, the use of the word *over*fishing in relation to food supply is an example of anthropocentrism as noted in the data analysis. However, the non-questioning of the *over* in overfishing creates a further tension in trying to move toward creating new understandings of food security, because the origins of the problem are not being questioned or asked to be unpacked through the content (this is not in relation to what the instructor is or would do in the classroom). This inconsistency could also be seen as a cyclical scenario in which solutions to problems are created but they do not address the root of the problem. Some food security/systems scholars, such as Garnett (2013) and Sage (2012) are asking for a break in this thinking, and for the creation of solutions that get to the root of the problem. As a result of this *same way of doing things*, the *same solutions* are being proposed. A suggested way of addressing this cycle is to examine the intentions behind the solutions being proposed. Or in other words, it is imperative to develop an understanding that "the way we frame a problem determines the ways we try to solve it" (Tesh, 1988, as cited in Power, 2009, p. 35). Additionally, from a theoretical standpoint, the lack of going deeper in the analysis is working against an EcoJustice understanding of the topic of food security/insecurity. The opposition toward the aims of the theory is shown through not questioning the *over* within curricular excerpts. This lack of questioning leaves the analysis incomplete because the roots of the thinking are not unpacked to understand the origins. Consequently, moving forward in the pursuit of integration of the topic stays at an in-between level of understanding regarding the thought-to-action connection advanced by EcoJustice Education.

CONCLUSIONS

There is still much to be learned about how integration is and could take place within teacher education programs in Ontario. Through the process of designing this study and examining data through interviews and document reviews, I was able to reflect and conclude on steps taken and where the possibilities could be for research on this topic.

To reiterate, the data showed no connection (aside from one faculty of education) between the overall program planning and instruction, as there is no observed direct line of support or level of intention in the programming of the topic at the program level. Additionally, the data shows through the participants' teaching that the topic is integrated in different subject areas, although what is emerging is a leaning toward topical integration through EE coursework. The observation of EE as an emerging course of choice for integration opens the question of EE being a suitable place for integration at this current time. The occurrence of the topic of food security throughout several curricular areas—those occurrences being in concentrations in only some subject areas (e.g. Social Studies and Humanities) further creates a picture of understanding the topic of food security to be non-holistic. This result is counter to the intention of the theoretical framing I used, which is to have a holistic understanding created through and across subject areas.

A concrete reasoning for such a picture or stage of integration could be based on various aspects, such as the complexity of the topic similar to a challenge for integration of EE in teacher education, to a lack of know-how toward integration experienced in teacher education programs (Liu, 2009).

The second finding, which I consider being part of the overall integration of the topic, is taking place by teacher educators across different faculties of education. The integration demonstrates the use of strategies encouraged by the theory of EcoJustice Education—which are the use of community-based learning, cultural ecological analysis and developing a global/local outlook on an issue. The findings within the context of overall integration illustrated that programming (e.g. through the program overviews) does not influence (although it is seen as a challenge in EE through a lack of commitment at the institutional level, see Babiuk et al., 2010) or did not appear to affect integration. Moreover, the organizational focus of the faculties of education where participants work did not show evidence of hindering integration. Posing the question to participants about the influence of the organizational focus pushed them to think about the actual *organizational focus* of the faculty within which they work. However, in all instances, it is apparent through the participants' words, and through a general observation throughout the interviews, that participants are being supported in their endeavors for integration. I showed through the excerpts from interviews that the participants reflect a connection between thought, language (descriptions given) and actions. The evidence I presented reflects an EcoJustice way of building awareness and understanding of an issue through teaching. The finding illustrates that the theory of EcoJustice Education offers a platform to change the way the concept of food security is conceptualized, and the way the topic is taught in teacher education.

Challenges to integration did not surface as a main obstacle to all participants, rather challenges appeared to be somewhat part of the process of integration and were not consistently experienced by teacher educators. There is no uniformity at this point in challenges, which is articulated through the interviews. The challenge to recruitment of participants for my study could also reflect a challenge to integration in the teacher education programs.

The last finding uncovers the perspectives that underpin integration practices. My study demonstrated that across all the data, there is the prominence of ways of thinking belonging to Sustainable Cultures. Thus, this part of the findings suggests a movement toward a systemic approach to integration by being present through a participant's thoughts and instruction as well as in their description of instruction. Moreover, these ways of thinking are seen or are ways of thinking which are present in thoughts, language use and actions that are demonstrative of more positive actions toward the planet. The perspectives, which reflect those of Western Modern Cultures, are only contained within the curriculum documents. Given the fact that participants did not directly use the curriculum documents, makes it difficult to conclude the role (or effect) of curriculum documents upon integration practices.

These concluding remarks trigger reflections and inquiries upon the integration practices of the concept of food security in teacher education programs in the field of EE. It is evident that EE serves as a platform through the characteristics of the field itself, and as further evidenced through the example of strategies used in this study by participants that are situating their work in EE. The mention of a designated EE course is neither to suggest that the other strategies are not grounded in EE nor to prescribe the type of course upon which integration is to occur. Additionally, the data analyzed in this study demonstrates an alignment with the use of EcoJustice Education as a theoretical framing for integration. The alignment showed a focus upon language use, as well as the presence or absence of attention paid toward the connections between intention of the teacher educator and design (of instruction) which can help to bring awareness to what is being conveyed through teaching on the topic of food security.

IMPLICATIONS FOR INTEGRATION

In this section, I outline implications for integration on the topic of food security in teacher education programs. By integration, I am referring to the embedding of the topic of food security as part of teacher education programs. The reference to integration mirrors the work of Evans et al.'s (2017) study in which the authors sought to investigate what approaches to embedding sustainability are occurring in teacher education. To reiterate, my interest in integration for this study was based on surveying what was happening at the program and at the classroom level. More specifically, my focus was on several aspects of teacher education programs, such as what practices are in place, what approaches are being used, and what perspectives are guiding integration practices. From the analysis, I composed several suggestions that could assist in the furthering of integration in teacher education programs. I conceive of these suggestions to be broadly conceptualized and broadly implemented, that is how they are enacted in teacher education programs will vary based on the context within each program. The suggestions are shaped by the literature review and the theoretical framing of EcoJustice Education and are the following: (1) A systemic approach to integration at the program level; (2), An integrated (cross-curricular) approach to teaching the topic of food security: The creation of a thematic based workshop; (3) The use of community-based learning, cultural ecological analysis, and developing a global/local outlook as strategies for the integration of the topic of food security; (4) The development of a more specific set of challenges that comprise the integration of the topic of food security; and (5) Develop policy initiatives through public dialogue between teacher education programs.

A Systemic Approach to Integration at the Program Level

For the first implication, I am putting forward the idea of having the topic of food security integrated across the teacher education program. In other words, the topic becomes part of a core focus on practices and policies within an overall teacher education program. This suggestion mirrors Evans et al.'s (2017) belief in how sustainability could be embedded into teacher education programs. With the noted challenges outlined in the integration of EE, and the commencement of collecting challenges described by participants in this study, working toward a systemic approach may alleviate some of the challenges, as well as lay the groundwork for integration. The suggestion is not to add to an overburdened workload within teacher education programs, but to drive the point that food security and, more broadly, food are imperative issues that teacher education can address. As I outlined in the methodology and results sections of this study, there is a hesitancy in integration. Having the topic integrated in a more interconnected manner could present itself through linking the programming with instruction, for instance. The suggestion I am putting forth is not to be seen or enacted as a prescription or directive for how integration is to take place, wherein there becomes a lack of autonomy on the part of teacher educators' practices, but to demonstrate institutional support.

The Creation of a Thematic Based Workshop

As evidenced by the review of curriculum documents, the concentrated and specific mention of the topic of food security is contained within the *Social Studies and Humanities* subject area. Moreover, there are additional topical pieces spread out in different subject-based areas which cause a disconnected understanding of the topic. To remedy what can appear to be seen as "silos" toward a more holistic approach to integration of the topic of food security is the facilitation of a workshop for teacher educators. The workshop is around the centralized theme of food security and acts as a space for teacher educators to learn how to interweave their subject matter knowledge with other subject matter backgrounds through collaborating with teacher educators.[2]

This strategy refers to the strengths model of integration used in EE. The strengths model of integration focuses on the integration of sustainability using disciplines as a starting point. The strengths rest in the subject matter background of teacher educators within teacher education programs. Each teacher educator, through their discipline specialty, can contribute to infusing sustainability into preservice teacher training. The strengths approach is seen as a step before classroom-based practices of integrating sustainability instead of having to retrain in-service teachers. Teacher education programs utilizing such an approach can train new teachers to identify and recognize the ways in which the specific disciplines they teach can contribute to a holistic approach to sustainability education (McKeown-Ice & Hopkins, 2002). Utilizing this strategy could work to alleviate some of the noted challenges mentioned in my study gleaned from teacher educators and outlined in my review of the literature. For instance, challenges which could be addressed through the workshop are a lack of resources (in this case the collaboration amongst teacher educators can act as a resource), variances in understandings of concepts such as food security and lack of know-how (as in an actual strategy) for integration.

Strategies for the Integration of the Topic of Food Security

The strategies outlined by the participants in my study appear to be useful ways of integrating the topic into teacher education. I suggest a continuation of the use of these strategies. Community-based learning, as I previously mentioned, calls for learning about the place in which one lives by going out into the community. From an EcoJustice perspective, this strategy adds the critical standpoint of working to ameliorate conditions within one's community that are seen as counter to ecological and social justice. In addition, I suggest the use of a learning garden as part of community-based learning. The use of a learning garden, as stated by Williams and Brown (2012) assists in building knowledge of food-related issues such as food security and sustainability. This method of fostering learning on such topics, according to DiGiuseppe et al. (2016), is occurring within a teacher education program in Ontario where part of this type of learning is based on working with community members, Elders, and experts in the fields of nature conversation, journalism, and community gardening.

The second strategy I suggest should continue is the development of cultural ecological analysis through language analysis. To reiterate, cultural ecological analysis is about learning that the ecological and social issues the planet faces have intertwined cultural roots based on ways of thinking reflective of Western Modern Cultures. A way to reveal these connections is through analyzing language. For instance, teacher training for teacher educators and teacher candidates can focus on the analysis of perspectives that are embedded within curriculum documents and other resources used for instruction on food security. The analysis completed in this study is an example of analyzing language used by participants, and in the documents used by teacher educators in their respective teaching practices. To accomplish this process, one can refer to the methodology I outline in this study (I utilized the perspectives as outlined in the text EcoJustice Education) as well as a text by Rita Turner (2015), titled *Teaching for EcoJustice*, which shows how (through a creation of a lesson) to analyze for perspectives embedded in language. The lesson to which I am referring is not specifically on food security, however, the outlining of lessons is useful as a starting point for this activity.

Lastly, I suggest the continuation of developing a global/local outlook of understanding the topic of food security as a teaching strategy. The use of this strategy is vital in developing the knowledge needed to grasp the complex and interwoven connections that exist currently regarding the global food system, and to the causes and effects of food insecurity experienced among and within nations as exhibited in the literature review of this study.

Developing a Specific Set of Challenges

Based on the research presented in this study, there is evidence of teacher educators working to implement the topic of food security in teacher education programs through the field of EE across Ontario. Additionally, through this research, there are documented challenges to integration that align with some of the challenges outlined in the related literature on approaches to embedding sustainability across teacher education programs. From a review of the most recent polygraph published by the Canadian Association of Teacher Education in 2017, there is clear evidence of work being done in initial teacher education programs on the topic of EE. However, there is limited discussion on the topic of EcoJustice, and an absence of the discussion on the topic of food security. Consequently, I suggest the development of a set of challenges to integration on the topic of food security in teacher education programs developed by teacher educators and administration within faculties of education. The set of challenges is to act as a form of proactive strategies for future integration which can serve to contribute to the work currently being done in teacher education programs.

Develop Policy Initiatives

I suggest the Association of Canadian Deans of Education (2018) help ensure that teacher education programs enact Principle 3 of the Accord on Teacher education, as there is no current accord on food security or the interrelated issue of climate change, for instance. In particular, I am referring to the aspect of the principle, which states that a professional teacher education program "understands and promotes a socio-ecologically just and environmentally literate society" (p. 2). As I demonstrated above, the pressing issue of food security and food insecurity are issues that require such a consideration. Moreover, the issues require teacher education programs to act to address these pressing problems as part of the transformative learning potential of teacher education programs to "foster an inclusive and equitable society" (p. 2) as articulated by the Association of Canadian Deans of Education. To accomplish this suggestion, the

Association of Canadian Deans of Education can create policy initiatives that promote professional development in teacher education programs on the integration of the topic of food security (aside from the promotion of workshops mentioned as another suggestion). Further, the Association of Canadian Deans of Education can provide opportunities for dialogue amongst its members to discuss the potentialities of integration, and the challenges to integration with faculties of education, in collaboration with the directors of teacher education programs.

CONTRIBUTIONS TO THE LITERATURE

Overall, my study adds to research in the fields of food systems and food security, environmental and teacher education. In terms of the fields of food systems and food security, I have added to the work by Berry et al. (2015), Garnett (2014), and Sage (2012) on the interconnections between food security and sustainability by focusing on the integration of food security as an environmental and sustainability related issue to be explored in education. More specifically, I have contributed to existing research on the subset of work that focuses on education as a way forward to address food and food security (broadly conceived) by gaining insights from educators, in particular teacher educators' views on the integration of food and food security in teacher education.

In terms of the field of environmental education, my study adds to the conversation of food and the environment by adding the concept of food security to existing discussions on food related aspects documented in the research (on food and EE). This research also makes a timely contribution to the field of teacher education within EE, because research on the role of teacher education demonstrates the influence teacher education can have in addressing pressing sustainability issues, such as food security. Due to the novelty of this study, I leaned upon existing research on approaches to embed EE in teacher education as a background to understand and examined the current integration practices and challenges toward integration on the topic of food security in teacher education programs.

The design of this study serves as a test of the playing field in terms of finding out what is occurring in teacher education programs when it comes to integration, and mirrors studies conducted in Australia (Buchanan, 2012) and in the United States (Ashmann & Franzen, 2017) on documenting types of integration practices (although these studies are on EE integration). There is also research by Elsden-Clifton and Futter-Puati (2015) conducted in Australia, and Young and Stanley's (2018) work conducted in Canada, which exhibit approaches to integration that are interventionist in nature, meaning the documented accounts of integration are experienced by the researcher. In my study, I outline integration practices on the topic of food security as described by the participants as to what is occurring in their own teaching practices.

The use of document reviews as part of the design of my study shows the current state of integration on the topic of food security across curriculum and policy documents in Ontario. Moreover, the examination of the documents provides a snapshot of what is presented on the topic, and in what subject-based content areas. The result, in turn acts as a reference point for current and future integration on the topic for teacher educators, as well as provides a collective representation of content within EE. Subsequently, this research contributes to documenting food security education and EE in the context of Ontario teacher education programs.

This study adds to the limited research on food education from the perspective of EcoJustice Education. To this point, the findings of this study contribute to building an understanding of food security as an issue of EcoJustice as advanced by scholars such as Shiva (2005), Martusewicz et al. (2011) and Lupinacci and Happel-Parkins (2018). Research on the use of integration strategies, for instance, demonstrates the use of school gardens as a way of understanding food related issues. The results of my study advance additional and specific integration strategies to address the topic of food security, such as community-based learning, cultural ecological analysis, and fostering a global/local understanding. Also, part of the theory of EcoJustice Education is about understanding the connections between language, thought, and action. My study adds to this imperative as shown through research by Kulnieks et al. (2012) and Young and Stanley (2018) by designing and examining not only individuals' understanding of food security but by trying to discover the perspectives guiding the integration practices of the topic in teacher education programs. The significance of understanding the underlying perspectives—that is, the way food security is conceptualized and enacted through education adds additional perspectives on food security as understood through education. Incorporating additional perspectives on the topic of food security further advances the work of several food systems and food security scholars, such as Fullbrook (2010), Garnett (2014), and Shiva (2013). These scholars put forth the notion that to move forward toward more sustainable food security, there is the requirement for new values and paradigms to take place. My study provides ways of thinking from the field of environmental education, which further concretizes the role of education in bringing forward a new engagement with food.

Lastly, this work could be relevant to other disciplines, such as life sciences, agricultural studies, and health and nutrition. The usefulness of this work rests in acting as an example of how to analyze language use in educational resources, also as a way to explore how concepts like sustainability, food security and the environment are conceptualized in these classroom settings.

LIMITATIONS AND DELIMITATIONS OF THE STUDY

There are some limitations to the design of my study. The manner in which I was able to recruit participants limited the pool of participants from which I was able to select for an interview. My initial intention was to recruit participants within a faculty of education by sending out a recruitment text that would reach multiple participants at once. A method such as this could reach a larger group of potential participants, and participants would then be selected on a first come first serve basis. Upon my initial recruiting, it was evident that this process was not favoured by all faculties, and I would require additional ethics procedures. At this point, to continue with recruitment, I searched by individual participant's information presented on the school's website for recruitment. The information available was not always consistent, meaning that some participants had enough information to meet the criteria for my study, whereas others did not have enough information available for me to discern if they fit the criteria. The situation may have limited the pool of participants from which to select, and therefore limited the number of potential participants.

The small sample size limited the descriptions and perspectives I was able to collect on integration practices. Therefore, I was not able to concretely begin to form a pattern or trend of a certain type of integration strategy on the topic of food security occurring across teacher education programs.

The lack of prior research on my topic posed a limitation regarding situating my findings within previous studies on the integration of the topic of food security in teacher education. As a result, the findings of my study are situated within related literature on the integration of EE in teacher education and can only be presented as in relation to current research on the intersection of food and EE. Therefore, there is room for improvement in refining and developing future research studies on the topic under investigation in this study.

Lastly, there is the potentiality that other ways of understanding food security could have been overlooked because they did not fit in the discourses outlined from the theory of EcoJustice Education, such as through language associated with Sustainable and/or Western Modern Cultures. In other words, advocating for EcoJustice or thinking about food security can be evidenced by words that are not shown by languages already in use. Consequently, this study may have not captured the entirety of perspectives or potentialities of ways of thinking in relation to food security, whether they would be positive or detrimental toward the planet.

My study also had some delimitations. I designed this study to look at integration practices in Ontario, as such the insights I gained only capture what is occurring in Ontario in terms of integration.

This research focused on the descriptions given by teacher educators rather than on observation of classroom practices. My focus was on the language and perspectives used when participants spoke and thought about their integration practices within their respective teacher education programs. Moreover, my study focused on how food security as a concept is taken up within documents and used by teacher educators, and how the constructions of food security are mediated within program planning and teaching practices. Therefore, had I focused on classroom practices of integration, perhaps I could have studied any interactions which may have affected or widen the lens of interpretation of integration practices.

FUTURE RESEARCH

The results of my study, and the current state of research on the intersections between food, EE and teacher education, open several possibilities for future research. I outline below several possibilities to continue the exploration of integration practices for the topic of food security:

1. Explore integration practices in teacher education programs across Canada. A study like this could offer a pan-Canadian view of the research problem that formed this study. The results from multiple studies would allow not only for a documentation of practices but offer comparative data through examining similarities or differences in types of strategies used, as well as successes and challenges toward integration.
2. Design a study on the actual use of curriculum documents by teacher educators in their integration practices. Conducting such a study could show how teacher educators interpret documents used in their teaching, as well as reveal direct connections between how the concept is presented in text to how the interpretations unfold in actual practice. As part of this study, an additional piece could be to explore the specificity in location of the teacher educator in relation to the use and interpretation of the curriculum documents for their respective integration practices. That is, by exploring the specificity of the teacher educator, one can gain more insight into the influence of lived experiences on their interactions with the curriculum documents.

3. Conduct a historical analysis of the evolution of the Ontario curriculum documents used in this study to examine political shifts in the inclusion or not of the topic of food and food-related aspects, as outlined in this research. Although this was not conducted for this study, the results of a historical analysis could indicate patterns of influences and political shifts that led or could lead to further inclusion of the topic.

Reflecting upon the original questions posed to me during the beginning stages of this research project, I reiterate the imperative of continuing the path toward attaining sustainable food security. Environmental education as a field of study and in particular teacher education are vital places to foster further inquiry into understanding the ways in which integration of the topic can take place. Moreover, teacher education programs can reach many avenues for change such as curriculum and policy development, classroom practices and to the communities in which educators and learners belong. The choice of trying to raise awareness and broaden knowledge about food security through EcoJustice Education aligns with the researchers' and my interest in teaching strategies that push educators and learners to unpack why things are the way they are—through our thoughts, language use and behaviours toward food and the planet.

ENDNOTES

1. Andree's (2007) study is not in the field of teacher education, although the scholar utilizes a pedagogical theory to frame the work.
2. The workshop would also provide opportunities for collaborations on curricula integration (this suggestion is based on the research by Collins-Figuoera's (2012) work on biodiversity education as mentioned in the literature view of this study).

REFERENCES

Ackerman-Leist, P. (2013). *Rebuilding the foodshed: How to create local, sustainable, and secure food systems.* Chelsea Green Publishing.

Ahlberg, M., Aanismaa, P., & Dillion, P. (2005). Education for sustainable living: Integrating theory, practice, design, and development. *Scandinavian Journal of Educational Research, 49*(2), 167–186. https://doi.org/10.1080/00313830500048923

Aleixandre, M. P. J., & Gayoso, I. G.-R. (1996). An approach to introducing environmental education into the science methods course in teacher education. *Environmental Education Research, 2*(1), 27–38.

Alexandratos, N., & Bruinsma, J. (2012). *World agriculture towards 2030/2050: The 2012 revision.* ESA Working paper No. 12-03. FAO. http://www.fao.org/fileadmin/templates/esa/Global_persepctives/world_ag_2030_50_2012_rev.pdf

Allen, P. (2013). Facing food security. *Journal of Rural Studies, 29*, 135–138. https://doi.org/10.1016/j.jrurtud.2012.12.002

Allen, P., FitzSimmons, M., Goodman, M., & Warner, K. (2003). Shifting plates in the agrifood landscape: The tectonics of alternative agrifood initiatives in California. *Journal of Rural Studies, 19*(1), 61–75. http://doi.org/ 10.1016/S0743-0167(02)00047-5

Alsop, S. Dippo, D., & Zandvliet, D. B. (2007). Teacher education as or for social and ecological transformation: Place-based reflections on local and global participatory methods and collaborative practices. *Journal of Education for Teaching, 33*(2), 207–223. https://doi.org/10.1080/02607470701259499

Andrée, P. (2007). The food bank as classroom: Community-based education for teaching and social change. *New Community Quarterly, 5*(2), 45–51.

Ardoin, N. M., Clark, C., & Kelsey, E. (2012). An exploration of future trends in environmental education research. *Environmental Education Research,* 1–22. http://doi.org/ 10.1080/13504622.2012.709823

Ashmann, S., & Franzen, R. L. (2017). In what ways are teacher candidates being prepared to teach about the environment? A case study from Wisconsin. *Environmental Education Research, 23*(3), 299–323. http://doi.org/10.1080/13504622.2015.1101750

Association of the Canadian Deans of Education. (2018). *Accord on teacher education.* http://csse-scee.ca/acde/wp-content/uploads/sites/7/2018/05/Accord-on-Teacher-Education.pdf

Auger, W. F., & Rich, S. J. (2007). *Curriculum theory and methods: Perspectives on learning and teaching.* Wiley.

Babiuk, G., Falkenberg, T., Deer, F., Giesbrecht, S., & Singh, S. (2010). *Sustainable development and living through changing teacher education and teaching in Manitoba.* Canadian Council on Learning. https://home.cc.umanitoba.ca/~falkenbe/Publications/Research_Report_(Babiuk_Falkenberg).pdf

Barth, M., Michelsen, G., Rieckmann, M., & Thomas, I. (Eds.). (2016). *Routledge handbook of higher education for sustainable development.* Routledge.

Bateson, G. (1972). *Steps to an ecology of mind: Collected essays in anthropology, psychiatry, evolution, and epistemology.* Chandler.

Bazeley, P., & Jackson, K., (2013). *Qualitative data analysis with NVIVO.* SAGE.

Beaumont, P. (2020). Millions hang by a thread: Extreme global hunger compounded by Covid-19. *The Guardian.* https://www.theguardian.com/global-development/2020/apr/21/millions-hang-by-a-thread-extreme-global-hunger-compounded-by-covid-19-coronavirus

Beckford, C. (2008). Re-orienting environmental education in teacher education programs in Ontario. *Journal of Teaching and Learning, 5*(1), 55–66.

Beddington, J. R., Asaduzzaman, M., Clark, M. E., Fernández Bremauntz, A., Guillou, M. D., Jahn, M. M., Lin, E., Mamo, T., Negra, C., Nobre, C. A., Scholes, R. J., Sharma, R., Van Bo, N., & Wakhungu, J. (2012). The role for scientists in tackling food insecurity and climate change. *Agriculture & Food Security, 1*(10), 1–9. https://doi.org/10.1186/2048-7010-1-10

Behjat, A. (2016). *Exploring the geography of food deserts and potential association with obesity in rural British Columbia* [Doctoral dissertation, University of Victoria, British Columbia]. https://dspace.library.uvic.ca/handle/1828/7658

Benn, J. (2014). Food, nutrition or cooking literacy—a review of concepts and competencies regrading food education. *International Journal of Home Economics, 7*(1), 13–35. https://pure.au.dk/portal/files/81132625/food_literacy.pdf

Berezowitz, C. K., Bontrager, A. B., & Schoeller, D. A. (2015). School gardens enhance academic performance and dietary outcomes in children. *Journal of School Health, 85*, 508–518. http://doi.org/10.1111/josh.12278

Berry, E. M., Dernini, S., Burlingame, B., Meybeck, A., & Conforti, P. (2015). Food security and sustainability: Can one exist without the other? *Public Health Nutrition, 18*(13), 2293–2302. http://doi.org/10.1017/S136898001500021X

Blay-Palmer, A. (2010). *Imagining sustainable food systems: Theory and practice.* Ashgate.

Blay-Palmer, A., Knezevic, I., & Spring, A. (2014). Seeking common ground for food system transformation. *Dialogues in Human Geography, 4*(2), 185–189. http://doi.org/10.1177/2043820614537154

Bloch, G. (2014, January 27). As a doctor, I know too well why the minimum wage needs to rise. *The Globe and Mail.* http://www.theglobeandmail.com/globe-debate/as-a-doctor-i-know-too-well-why-the-minimum-wage-needs-to-rise/article16516712

Born, B., & Purcell, M., (2006). Avoiding the local trap: Scale and food systems in planning research. *Journal of Planning Education and Research 26*, 195–207. http://doi.org/10.1177/0739456X06291389

Bortolin, K. (2013). *Community-based learning in teacher education: Toward a situated understanding of ESL learners* [Doctoral Dissertation, University of Victoria]. https://www.collectionscanada.gc.ca/obj/thesescanada/vol2/BVIV/TC-BVIV-4863.pdf

Bowers, C. A. (1993). *Education, cultural myths, and the ecological crisis: Toward deep changes.* State University of New York Press.

Bowers, C. A. (1997). *The culture of denial: Why the environmental movement needs a strategy for reforming universities and public schools.* State of University of New York Press.

Bowers, C. A. (2001a). *Educating for eco-justice and community.* University of Georgia Press.

Bowers, C. A. (2001b). Toward an eco-justice pedagogy. *Environmental Education Research, 8*(1), 21–34. http://doi/org/10.1080/13504620120109628

Bowers, C. A. (2006). *Revitalizing the commons: Cultural and educational sites of resistance and affirmation.* Rowman & Littlefield.

Bowers, C. A. (2009a). Educating for a revitalization of the cultural commons. *Canadian Journal of Environmental Education, 14,* 196–200. https://files.eric.ed.gov/fulltext/EJ842749.pdf

Bowers, C. A. (2012a). *The way forward: Educational reforms that focus on the cultural commons and the linguistic roots of the ecological/cultural crises.* Ecojustice Press.

Bowers, C. A. (2012b). Gregory Bateson's contribution to understanding the linguistic roots of the ecological crisis. *The Trumpeter, 28*(1), 8–42. http://trumpeter.athabascau.ca/index.php/trumpet/article/view/1276/1615

Bowers, C. A., & Flinders, D. J. (1990). *Responsive teaching: An ecological approach to classroom patterns of language, culture and thought.* Teachers College Press.

Breunig, M. (2013). Food for thought: An analysis of pro-environmental behaviours and food choices in Ontario Environmental studies programs. *Canadian Journal of Environmental Education, 18,* 155–172. https://cjee.lakeheadu.ca/article/view/1230/680

Bringle, R. G., & Hatcher, J. A. (1996). Implementing service learning in higher education. *The Journal of Higher Education, 67*(2), 221–239.

Britneff, B. (2020). Food banks' demand surges amid Covid-19. Now they worry about long-term pressures. *Global News.* https://globalnews.ca/news/6816023/food-bank-demand-covid-19-long-term-worry/

Brown, L. R. (2004). *Outgrowing the earth: The food security challenge in an age of falling water tables and rising temperatures.* W.W. Norton.

Brown, L. R. (2012a). The world is closer to a food crisis that most people realise. *The Guardian.* http://www.theguardian.com/environment/2012/jul/24/world-food-crisis-closer

Brown, L. R. (2012b). *Full planet, empty plates: The new geopolitics of food scarcity.* W.W. Norton.

Buchanan, J. (2012). Sustainability education and teacher education: Finding a natural habitat? *Australian Journal of Environmental Education, 28*(2), 108–124. http://doi.org/ 10.1017/aee.2013.4

Burke, G., & Cutter-Mackenzie, A. (2010). What's there, what if, what then, and what can we do? An immersive and embodied experience of environment and place through children's literature. *Environmental Education Research, 16*(3-4), 311–330. https://doi.org/10.1080/13504621003715361

Cajete, G. (1994). *Look to the mountain: An ecology of indigenous education.* Kivaki Press.

Campbell, A. M., & MacRae, R. (2013). Local food plus: The connective tissue in local/sustainable supply chain development. *Local Environment, 18*(5), 557–566. http://doi.org/10.1080/13549839.2013.788488

Canadian Biotechnology Action Network. (2019). *Human health risks.* https://cban.ca/gmos/issues/human-health-risks/

Capone, R., El Bilali, H., Debs, P., Cardone, G., & Driouech, N. (2014). Food system sustainability and food security: Connecting the dots. *Journal of Food Security, 2*(1), 13–22. http://doi.org/10.12691/jfs-2-1-2.

Carlsson, L., Williams, P. L. (2008). New approaches to the health promoting school: Participation in sustainable food systems. *Journal of Hunger & Environmental Nutrition 3*(4), 400–417. https://doi.org/10.1080/19320240802529243

Caron, N., & Plunkett-Latimer, J. (2022). *Canadian Income Survey: Food insecurity and unmet health care needs, 2018 and 2019* (Catalogue no. 75F002M). Statistics Canada. https://www150.statcan.gc.ca/n1/en/pub/75f0002m/75f0002m2021009-eng.pdf?st=4nh4rFof

Cheong, I. P. A. (2005). Educating pre-service teachers for a sustainable environment. *Asia-Pacific Journal of Teacher Education, 33*(1), 97–110. https://doi.org/10.1080/1359866052000341151

Clay E. (2002, July 11–12). Food Security: Concepts and Measurement [Paper presentation]. FAO Expert Consultation on Trade and Food Security: Conceptualizing the Linkages. (Published as "Chapter 2 Food security: Concepts and measurements," 2003, In FAO *Trade Reforms and Food Security: conceptualizing the linkages* (pp. 25–33), http://www.fao.org/3/a-y4671e.pdf

Cohen, M. J., & Garrett, J. L. (2009). *The food price crisis and urban food (in) security*. http://pubs.iied.org/pdfs/10574IIED.pdf

Collins-Figueora, M. (2012). Biodiversity and education for sustainable development in teacher education programmes of four Jamaican educational institutions. *Journal of Education for Sustainable Development, 6*(2), 253–267. https://doi.org/10.1177/0973408212475257

Committee on World Food Security. (2012). *Coming to terms with terminology food security, nutrition security, food security and nutrition, food and nutrition security,* Thirty-nine section. http://www.fao.org/docrep/meeting/026/MD776E.pdf

Coppolino, A. (2016, Jan, 22). Back to basics: Children need to learn about food. *CBC News.* http://www.cbc.ca/news/canada/kitcher-waterloo/back-to-basics-children-need-to-learn-about-food-1.3413776

Council for Biotechnology Information. (2018). *Health and safety concerns.* https://gmoanswers.com/health-safety-consensus-0

Council of Canadian Academies. (2014). *Aboriginal food security in Northern Canada: An assessment of the state of knowledge.* Council of Canadian Academies. https://cca-reports.ca/wp-content/uploads/2018/10/foodsecurity_fullreporten.pdf

Crosley, K. L. (2013). Advancing the boundaries of urban environmental education through the food justice movement. *Canadian Journal of Environmental Education, 18*, 1–13. https://cjee.lakeheadu.ca/article/view/1257/672

Dallimore, E., Rochefort, D. A., & Simonelli, K. (2010). Community-based learning and research. *New Directions for Teaching and Learning, 124*, 15–22. https://doi.org/10.1002/tl.416

Davila, F., & Dyball, R. (2015). Transforming food systems through food sovereignty: An Australian urban context. *Australian Journal of Environmental Education, 31*(1), 34–45. http://doi.org/10.1017/aee.2015.14

Dawe, G., Jucker, R., & Martin, S. (2005). *Sustainable development in higher education: Current practices and future developments*. Higher Education Academy. https://www.heacademy.ac.uk/system/files/sustdevinHEfinalreport.pdf

Delaney, T., & Madigan, T. (2014). *Beyond sustainability: A thriving environment*. McFarland.

Denzin, N. K., & Lincoln, Y. S. (2011). Introduction: The discipline and practice of qualitative research. In N. K. Denzin, & Y. S. Lincoln (Eds.), *The SAGE handbook of qualitative research* (pp. 1–20). SAGE.

De Roux-Smith, I. (2014). *Foodbanks, food drives, and food insecurity: The social construction of hunger* [Master of Social Work Thesis, McMaster University]. https://macsphere.mcmaster.ca/bitstream/11375/16400/1/Food%20Banks_Food%20Drives_Food%20Insecurity_MSW_thesis_Iris%20De%20Roux-Smith_FINAL.pdf

De Schutter, O. (2012). *Visit to Canada from 6 to 16 May 2012. Mandate of the Special Rapporteur on the right to food*. United Nations Office of the United Nations High Commissioner for Human Rights. http://www.srfood.org/images/stories/pdf/officialreports/201205_canadaprelim_en.pdf

Dewey, J. (1974). *Experience and education*. Collier Books.

Dhawan, S. (2014). Food security: Awareness among the pupil teachers. *Indian Stream Research Journal, 3*(12), 1–5.

Dieterle, J. M. (2015). *Just food: Philosophy, justice and food*. Rowman & Littlefeld.

DiGiuseppe, M., Elliott, P., Ibrahim Khan, S., Rhodes, S., Scott, J., & Steele, A. (2016). Rising to the challenge: Promoting environmental education in three Ontario faculties of education. In D. D. Karrow, M. DiGiuseppe, P. Elliott, Y. Gwekewerere, & H. Inwood (Eds.), *Canadian perspectives on initial teacher environmental education praxis* (pp. 92–127). Canadian Association for Teacher Education (CATE).

Dinshaw, F. (2016, June 1). Climate change threatens to turn Prairies into dust bowl; Canadians should consider actions against weather-related risks. *Chronicle-Herald, A3*.

Dupuis, E. M., & Goodman, D. (2005). Show we go "home to eat?: Toward a reflexive politics of localism. *Journal of Rural Studies, 21*(3), 359–371. https://doi.org/10.1016/j.jrurstud.2005.05.011

Earl, L. (2018). *Schools and food education in the 21st century*. Routledge.

Elsden-Clifton, J., & Futter-Puati, D. (2015). Creating a health and sustainability nexus in food education: Designing third spaces in teacher education. *Australian Journal of Environmental Education, 31*(1), 86–98. https://doi.org/10.1017/aee.2014.44

Ericksen, P. J. (2008). Conceptualizing food systems for global environmental change. *Global Environmental Change, 18*(1), 234–245. https://doi.org/10.1016/j.gloenvcha.2007.09.002

Evans, N., Stevenson, R. B., Lasen, M., Ferreira, J., & Davis, J. (2017). Approaches to embedding sustainability in teacher education: A synthesis of literature. *Teaching and teacher education, 63*, 405–417. https://doi.org/10.1016/j.tate.2017.01.013

Evans, N., Whitehouse, H., & Hickey, R. (2012). Pre-service teachers' conceptions of education for sustainability. *Australian Journal of Teacher Education, 37*(7), 1–12. http://doi.org/10.14221/ajte.2012v37n7.3

Evans, P. (2017, June 19). Meat prices set to rise up to 9% this year even as other groceries take less of a bite. *CBC News*. https://www.cbc.ca/news/business/canada-food-inflation-2017-report-dalhousie-researchers-1.4166923

Evans, T. L. (2012). *Occupy education: Living and learning sustainability*. Peter Lang.

Falkenburg, T., & Babiuk, G. (2014). The status of education for sustainability in initial teacher education programmes: A Canadian case study. *International Journal of Sustainability in Higher Education, 15*(4), 418–430. http://doi.org/10.1108/IJSHE-10-2012-0088

Falman, M. M., Dake, J. A., McCaughtry, N., & Martin, J. (2008). A pilot study to examine the effects of a nutrition intervention on nutrition knowledge, behaviours, and efficacy expectations in middle school children. *Journal of School Health, 78*(4), 216–222. http://doi.org/10.1111/j.1746-1561.2008.00289.x

Feagan, R. (2007). The place of food: Mapping out the 'local' in local food systems. *Progress in Human Geography, 31*(1), 23–42. https://doi.org/10.1177/0309132507073527

Fedoroff, N. V. (2015). Food in a future of 10 billion. *Agriculture & food security, 4*(11), 1–10. http://doi.org/10.1186/s40066-015-0031-7

Ferreira J., Ryan, L., Davis, J., Cavanagh, M., & Thomas, J. (2009). *Mainstreaming sustainability into pre-service teacher education in Australia*. The Australian Research Institute in Education for Sustainability for the Australian Government Department of the Environment, Water, Heritage and the Arts. http://aries.mq.edu.au/projects/preservice2/files/Pre-Service_Teacher_Ed2.pdf

Ferreira, J., Ryan, L., & Tilbury, D. (2006). *Whole-school approaches to sustainability: A review of models for professional development in pre-service teacher education*. Canberra: Australian Government Department of the Environment and Heritage and the Australian Research Institute inEducation for Sustainability (ARIES). http://www/aries.mq.edu.au/projects/preservice/files/TeacherEduDec06.pdf

Ferreira, J., Ryan, L., & Tilbury, D. (2007). Mainstreaming education for sustainable development in initial teacher education in Australia: A review of existing professional development models. *Journal of Education for Teaching, 33*(2), 225–239. https://doi.org/10.1080/02607470701259515

Firth, R., & Winter, C. (2007). Constructing education for sustainable development: The secondary school geography curriculum and initial teacher training. *Environmental Education Research, 13*(5), 599–619. https://doi.org/10/1080/13504620701659079.

Flowers, R., & Swan, E. (Eds.). (2016). *Food pedagogies*. Routledge.

Food and Agriculture Organization. (1996). *Declaration on world food security*. World Food Summit. http://www.fao.org/3/w3613e/w3613e00.htm

Food and Agriculture Organization. (2002). *Food insecurity: The state of food insecurity in the world 2001*. http://www.fao.org/3/y1500e/y1500e00.htm

Food and Agriculture Organization. (2003). *Trade reform and food security, Conceptualizing the linkages*. http://www.fao.org/3/a-y4671e.pdf

Food and Agriculture Organization. (2008). *An introduction of basic concepts of food security*. http://www.foodsec.org/pubs.htm

Food and Agriculture Organization. (2016). *The state of food and agriculture: Climate change, agriculture, and food security*. http://www.fao.org/3/a-i6030e.pdf

FAO, IFAD, UNICEF, WFP, & WHO. (2021). *The State of Food Security and Nutrition in the World 2021. Transforming food systems for food security, improved nutrition and affordable healthy diets for all*. Rome, FAO. https://doi.org/10.4060/cb4474en

Food Secure Canada (FSC). (n.d). *The launch of the first 'Food Policy for Canada-Everyone at the Table'*. https://foodsecurecanada.org/first-national-food-policy-for-canada

Ford, J. (2009). Vulnerability of Inuit food systems to food insecurity as a consequence of climate change: A case study from Igloolik, Nunavut. *Regional Environmental Change, 9*, 83–100. http://doi.org/10.1007/s10113-008-0060-x

Ford, J., MacDonald, J.P., Huet, C., Statham, S., & MacRury, A. (2016). Food policy in the Canadian North: Is there a role for country food markets? *Social Science & Medicine, 152*, 35–40. http://doi/org/10.1016/j.socscimed.2016.01.034

Foresight. (2011). *The Future of food and farming: Challenging and choices for global sustainability*. The Government Office for Science.

Frankenberger, T. R., & McCaston, M. K. (1998). *From food security to livelihood security: The evolution of concepts*. CARE.

Franklin, A., Newton, J., McEntree, J. C. (2011). Moving beyond the alternative: Sustainable communities, rural resistance and the mainstreaming of local food. *Local Environment, 16*(8), 771–778. https://doi.org/10.1080/13549839.2011.574685

Fraser, E., & Pascoal, S. (2015, September 23). A country that can't feed itself. *Toronto Star*. A17.

Fraser, S., & Chapin, L. (2017, March 14). Busting myths about food insecurity: Community gardens, subsidized housing not answers. *CBC News* http://www.cbc.ca/news/canada/prince-edward-island/pei-food-insecurity-tarasuk-doyle-upei-1.4024797

Fullbrook, D. (2010). Food as security. *Food Security, 2*, 5–20. http://doi.org/0.1007/s12571-009-0050-y

Gardner, B. (2013). *Global food futures: Feeding the world in 2050*. Bloomsbury.

Garnett, T. (2013). Food sustainability: problems, perspectives and solutions. *Proceeding of the Nutrition Society, 72*, 29–39. https://doi.org/10.1017/S0029665112002947

Garnett, T. (2014). Three perspectives on sustainable food security: efficiency, demand restraint, food system transformation. What role for LCA? *Journal of Cleaner Production, 73*(15), 10–18. http://doi.org/10.1016/j.jclepro.2013.07.045

George, J. (2020). Arctic conference considers the challenges posed by COVID-19. *Nunatsiaq News*. https://nunatsiaq.com/stories/article/covid-19-adds-new-layer-of-challenges-on-the-arctic-conference/

Godfray, H. C. J., Beddington, J. R., Crute, I. R., Haddad, L., Lawrence, D., Muir, J. F., Pretty, J., Robinson, S., Thomas, S. M., & Toulmin, C. (2010). Food security: The challenge of feeding 9 billion people. *Science, 327*, 812–817. http://doi.org/ 10.1126/science.1185383

Godrich, S. L., Davies, C. R., Darby, J., & Devine, A. (2017). What are the determinants of food security among regional and remote Western Australian children? *Australian and New Zealand Journal of Public Health, 4*(2), 172–177. http://doi.org/10.1111/1753-6405.12636

Gomiero, T., Pimental, D., & Paoletti, M. G. (2011). Is there a need for a more sustainable agriculture? *Critical Reviews in Plant Sciences, 30*, 6–23. https://doi.org/10.1080/07352689.2011.553515

Gooch, M., Felfel, A., & Marenick, N. (2010). *Food waste in Canada: Opportunities to increase the competitiveness of Canada's agri-food sector, while simultaneously improving the environment*. Value Chain Management Centre. http://vcm-international.com/wp-content/uploads/2013/04/Food-Waste-in-Canada-112410.pdf

Gorlewski, J., & Porfilio, B. J. (2012). Revolutionizing environmental education through Indigenous hip hop culture. *Canadian Journal of Environmental Education, 17*, 46–61.

Gottlieb, R., & Joshi, A. (2010). *Food justice*. The MIT Press.

Gough, A. (n.d.). *Not for want of trying: Strategies for re-orienting teacher education for Education for Sustainable Development* (ESD). https://citeseerx.ist.psu.edu/document?repid=rep1&type=pdf&doi=129a178c613ec8b5f052197d07e4cf0bdc482b18 http://citeseerx.ist.psu.edu/viewdoc/download?doi=10.1.1.504.6083&rep1&type=pdf

Gough, A. (2006, May 16). *Working at the margins of sustainability: Implementing ESD in Victorian government schools* [Seminar presentation] University of Bath Centre for Research in Education and the Environment, Bath, United Kingdom. http://www.bath.ac.uk/cree/resources/agoughESD2006paper.pdf

Gough, A. (2009). *Not for want of trying: Strategies for re-orienting teacher education for education for sustainable development (ESD)* [Paper presentation]. Asia-Pacific Program of Educational Innovation for Development, UNESCO Bangkok. http://citeseerx.ist.psu.edu/viewdoc/download?doi=10.1.1.504.6083&rep=rep1&type=pdf

Gough, A. (2013). *The emergence of environmental education research*: A "history" of the field. In R. B. Stevenson, M. Brody, J. Dillon, & A. E. J. Wals (Eds.), *International handbook of research on environmental education* (pp. 13–22). Routledge.

Government of Canada. (2019). *"Everyone at the Table!" Government of Canada announces the first-ever Food Policy for Canada*. https://www.canada.ca/en/agriculture-agri-food/news/2019/06/everyone-at-the-table-government-of-canada-announces-the-first-ever-food-policy-for-canada.html

Guest, G., Namey, E. E., & Mitchell, M. L. (Eds.). (2013). *Collecting qualitative data: A field manual for applied research*. SAGE.

Gustavsson, J., Cederberg, C., Sonesson, U., van Otterdijk, R., & Meybeck, A. (2011). *Global food losses and food waste: Extent, causes, and prevention*. Food and Agriculture Organization. http://www.fao.org/3/a-i2697e.pdf

Grant, T. (2012). Recession's legacy has food-bank usage soaring in Canada. *The Globe and Mail.* https://www.theglobeandmail.com/news/national/recessions-legacy-has-food-bank-usage-soaring-in-canada/article4748510/

Grant, T. (2014). Working for nothing: Canada joins minimum wage debate. *The Globe and Mail.* https://www.theglobeandmail.com/report-on-business/economy/working-for-nothing-canada-joins-global-minimum-wage-debate/article16508375/

Grant, T., & Blaze Baum, K. (2020). Ontario farms struggle to contain COVID-19 as migrant workers test positive. *The Globe and Mail.* https://www.theglobeandmail.com/canada/article-ontario-farms-struggle-to-contain- covid-19-as-migrant-workers-test/

Gruenewald, D. A. (2003). The best of both worlds: A critical pedagogy of place. *Educational Researcher, 32*(4), 3–12. http://www.jstor.org/stable/3700002

Gruenewald, D., & Smith, G. A. (2008). *Place-based education in the global age: Local diversity.* Lawrence Erlbaum Associates; Taylor & Francis Group.

Grote, U. (2014). Can we improve global food security? A socio-economic and political perspective. *Food Security, 6,* 187–200. http://doi.org/10.1007/s12571-013-0321-5

Hanchet, S. H. (2010). *Environmental education in Canadian Teacher Education* [Unpublished master's thesis]. Concordia University.

Hanson, C. (2013). *Food security, inclusive growth, sustainability, and the post-2015 development agenda: Background research paper.* World Resources Institute. https://www.post2020hlp.org/wp-content/uploads/docs/Hanson_Food-Security-Inclusive-Growth-Sustainability-and-the-Post-2015-Development-Agenda.pdf

Harris, C. E., & Barter, B. G. (2015). Pedagogies that explore food practices: Resetting the table for improved eco-justice. *Australian Journal of Environmental Education, 31*(1), 12–33. http://doi.org/10.1017/aee2015.12

Harris, K. (2020a). Food security experts warn of supply shortages, higher prices due to global pandemic. *CBC News.* https://www.cbc.ca/news/politics/food-security-covid19-trudeau-1.5520492

Harris, K. (2020b). Exploitation, abuse, health hazards rise for migrant workers during COVID-19, group says. *CBC News.* https://www.cbc.ca/news/politics/migrant-workers-farm-deaths-report-1.5602596

Health Canada. (2011). *Eating well with Canada's food guide.* http://publications.gc.ca/collections/collection_2012/sc-hc/H164-38-1-2011-eng.pdf

Heimlich, J., E., Braus, J., Olivolo, B., McKeown-Ice, R., & Barringer-Smith, L. (2004). Environmental Education and preservice teacher preparation: A National Study. *Journal of Environmental Education, 35*(2), 17–21. https://doi.org/10.3200/JOEE.35.2.17-60

Held, A. (2017, June 22). U.N. says world's population will reach 9.8 billion by 2050. *NPR*. http://www.npr.org/sections/thetwo-way/2017/06/22/533935054/u-n-says-world-s-population-will-reach-9-8-billion-by-2050

Hinrichs, C.C. (2000). Embeddedness and local food systems: Notes on two types of direct agricultural market. *Journal of Rural Studies, 16*(3), 295–303. https://doi.org/10.1016/S0743-0167(99)00063-7

Hinrichs, C.C. (2003). The practice and politics of food system localization. *Journal of Rural Studies, 19*, 33–45. http://doi.org/10.1016/S0743-0167(02)00040-2

Hoddinott, J. (1999). *Choosing outcome indicators of household food insecurity*. International Food Policy Research Institute. https://rmportal.net/framelib/choosing-outcome-indicators.pdf

Hoeg, D. G., & Barrett, S. E. (2016). Worldviews and preservice teachers' beliefs about nature and environmental education: A case for socially and culturally critical science teacher education (Ontario). In D. D. Karrow, M. DiGiuseppe, P. Elliott, Y. Gwekewerere, & H. Inwood (Eds.), *Canadian perspectives on initial teacher environmental education praxis* (pp. 36–66). Canadian Association for Teacher Education (CATE).

Holt-Giménez, E. (2011). Food security, food justice, or food sovereignty?: Crises, food movements and regime change. In A. H. Alkon, & J. Agyeman (Eds.), *Cultivating food justice: Race, class, and sustainability* (pp. 309–330). The MIT Press.

Hume, G. (2010). *The local food revolution*. Municipal World.

Hwalla, N., El Labban, S., & Bahn, R. A. (2016). Nutrition security is an integral component of food security. *Frontiers in Life Science, 9*(3), 167–172. https://doi.org/10.1080/21553769.2016.1209133

Ilbery, B., & Maye, D. (2005). Alternative (shorter) food supply chains and specialist livestock products in the Scottish-English borders. *Environment and Planning A, 37*(5), 823–844. https://doi.org/10.1068/a3717

Ingram, J. (2011). A food system approach to research food security to researching food security and its interactions with global environmental change. *Food Security, 3*, 417–431. http://doi.org/10.1007/s12571-011-0149-9

Inwood, H., Forbes, J., Di Giuseppe, M., Jagger, S., Cousineau, A., & Sperling, E. (2014). *Deepening environmental education in pre-service education resource*. Ontario Institute for Studies in Education.

Janhonen, K., Mäkelä, J., & Palojoki, P. (2016). Food education: From normative models to promoting agency. In *Learning, Food, and Sustainability* (pp. 93–110). Palgrave Macmillan.

Jarosz, L. (2009) The political economy of global governance and world food crisis: The case of the FAO. *Review: A Journal of the Fernand Braudel Center for the Study of Economies, Historical Systems, and Civilizations, 32*(1), 37–60.

Jarosz, L. (2014). Comparing food security and food sovereignty discourses. *Dialogues in Human Geography, 4*(2), 168–181. http://doi.org/10.1177/2043820614537161

Jenkins, K. (2000). Listening to secondary pre-service teachers: Implications for teacher education. *Australian Journal of Environmental Education, 15/16*, 49–56. (Original work published 1999)

Junker, R. (2004). Have the cake and eat it: Ecojustice versus development? Is it possible to reconcile social and economic equity, ecological sustainability and human development? Some implications for Ecojustice education. *Educational Studies: A Journal of the American Educational Studies Association, 36*(1), 10–25. https://doi.org/10.1207/s15326993es3601_3

Karpudewan, M., Ismail, Z. H., & Mohamed, N. (2009). The integration of green chemistry experiments with sustainable development concepts in pre-service teachers' curriculum. *International Journal of Sustainability in Higher Education, 10*(2), 118–135. http://doi.org/10.1108/14676370910945936

Kendrick, J. (2009). Commons thinking. In A. Stibbe (Ed.), *The handbook of sustainability literacy: Skills for a changing world* (pp. 51–57). Green Books.

Kirkpatrick, S. I., & Tarasuk, V. (2008). Food insecurity is associated with nutrient inadequacies among Canadian adults and adolescents. *The Journal of Nutrition Community and International Nutrition, 138*, 604–612. http://doi.org/ 10.1093/jn/138.3.604

Kissenger, M. (2013). Approaches for calculating nation's food ecological footprint—The case for Canada. *Ecological Indicators, 24*, 366–374. http://doi.org/10.1016/j.ecolind.2012.06.023

Koc, M., & MacRae, R., Desjardins, E., & Roberts, W. (2008). Getting civil about food: The interactions between civil society and the state to advance sustainable food systems in Canada. *Journal of Hunger and Environmental Nutrition, 3*(2–3), 122–144. http://doi.org/10.1080/19320240802243175

Koch, P. A. (2016). Learning, food, and sustainability in the school curriculum. In J. Sumner (Ed.), *Learning, food, and sustainability: Sites for resistance and change* (pp. 55–73). Palgrave Macmillan.

Korzun, M., & Webb, C. (2014). *Opportunities to fill the gaps in knowledge about the impacts of food education for children and youth in Ontario.* The Institute for Community Engaged Scholarship/Research Shop. http://www.theresearchshop.ca/resources

Kulnieks, A., Ng-A-Fook, N., Stanley, D., & Young, K. (2012). Reconsidering Canadian environmental curriculum studies: Framing an approach to ecojustice. In N. Ng-A-Fook & J. Rottmann (Eds.), *Reconsidering Canadian Curriculum Studies* (pp. 83–103). Palgrave MacMillan.

Kukaswadia, S. (2014, February 6). *Millions of working Canadians struggle to afford food: U of T report.* https://www.utoronto.ca/news/millions-working-canadians-struggle-afford-food-u-t-report

Lang, T., & Barling, D. (2012). Food security and food sustainability: Reformulating the debate. *The Geographical Journal, 178*(4), 313–326. http://doi.org/10.1111/j.1475-4959.2012.00480.x

Larsen, K., & Gilliland, J. (2009). A farmer's market in a food desert: Evaluating impacts on the price and availability of healthy food. *Health & Place, 15*, 1158–1162. http://doi.org/10.1016/j.healthplace.2009.06.007

Lawrence, G., Lyons, K., & Wallington, T. (2009). *Food security, nutrition and sustainability.* Routledge.

Lebel, A., Noreau, D., Tremblay, L., Oberlé, C., Girard-Gadreau, M., Duguay, M., Block, J.P. (2016). Identifying rural food deserts: Methodological considerations for food environment interventions. *Canadian Journal of Public Health, 107*(1), 21–26. http://doi.org/10.17269/CJPH.107.5353

Lee, A., McLeod-Kilmurray, & Chalifour, N. (2017, January 24). Canada's food guide update needs to address sustainability. *Policy Options.* http://www.policyoptions.irpp.org/magazines/january-2017/canadas-food-guide-update-needs-to-address-sustainability

Levkoe, C. Z. & Wilson, A. (2017, July 9th). The promise of a national food policy for Canada. *The Conversation.* http://www.theconversation.com/the-promise-of-a-national-food-policy-for-canada-80386

Lewis, L. H. & Williams, C. J. (1994). In L. Jackson, & R. S. Caffarella (Eds.), *Experiential Learning: A New Approach* (pp. 5–16). Jossey-Bass.

Lloro-Bidart, T. (2017). Neoliberal and disciplinary environmentality and 'sustainable seafood' consumption: Storying environmentally responsible action. *Environmental Education Research, 23*(8), 1182–1199. http://doi.org/10.1080/13504622.2015.1105198

Lin, E. (2002). Trend of environmental education in Canadian pre-service teacher education programs from 1979 to 1996. *Canadian Journal of Environmental Education, 7*(1), 199–215. https://pdfs.semanticscholar.org/f691/efd41b7798b5e750e82c2ec0ad0a4aa71201.pdf

Liu, J. (2009). Education for sustainable development in teacher education: Issues in the case of York University in Canada. *Asian Social Science, 5*(5), 46–49. https://pdfs.semanticscholar.org/b5a9/9c0df14bf71144b92e6a9b542a657dc4aade.pdf

Loopstra, R., & Tarasuk, V. (2015). Food bank usage is a poor indicator of food insecurity: Insights from Canada. *Social Policy & Society, 14*(3), 449–465. http://doi.org/10.1017/S1474746415000184

Lowenstein, E., Martusewicz, R., & Voelker, L. (2010). Developing teachers' capacity for EcoJustice Education and community-based learning. *Teacher Education Quarterly*, 99–118. https://files.eric.ed.gov/fulltext/EJ904903.pdf

Lupinacci, J. (2013). Eco-ethical environmental education: Critically and ethically examining our perceptions of being human. In A. Kulnieks, D. Roronhiakewen Longboat, & K. Young (Eds.), *Contemporary studies in environmental and indigenous pedagogies: A curricula of stories and place* (pp. 185–200). Sense.

Lupinacci, J., & Happel-Parkins, A. (2018). Food for a common(s) curriculum: Learning to recognize and resist food enclosures. In S. Rice & A. G. Rud (Eds.), *Educational dimensions of school lunch: Critical perspectives* (pp. 91–115). Palgrave.

MacRae, R. (2012). Food policy for the twenty-first century. In M. Koc, J. Sumner, J. & A. Winson (Eds.). *Critical perspectives in food studies* (pp. 310–323). Oxford University Press.

Malberg Dyg, P., & Wistoft, K. (2018). Wellbeing in school gardens: The case of the Gardens for Bellies food and environmental education program. *Environmental Education Research, 24*(8), 1177–1191.

Martusewicz, R. A., Edmundson, J., & Lupinacci, J. (2011). *Ecojustice education: Towards diverse, democratic, and sustainable communities*. Routledge.

Martusewicz, R. A., & Edmundson, J. (2005). Social foundations as pedagogies of responsibility and eco-ethical commitment. In D. Butin (Ed.), *Teaching context: A primer for the social foundations of education classroom* (pp. 71–92) Lawrence Elrbaum.

Maye, D., & Kirwan, J. (2013). Food security: A fractured consensus. *Journal of Rural Studies, 29*, 1–6.

Mayer-Smith, J., Bartosh, O., & Peterat, L. (2007). Teaming children and elders to grow food and environmental consciousness. *Applied Environmental Education and Communication, 6*, 77–85. http://doi.org/10.1080/15330150701319529

McIntyre, L., Patterson, P. B., Anderson, L. C., & Mah, C. L. (2016). Household food insecurity in Canada: Problem definition and potential solutions in the public policy domain. *Canadian Public Policy, 42*(1), 83–93. http://doi.org/10.3138/cpp.2015-066

McKeown-Ice, R. (2000). Environmental education in the United States: A survey of preservice teacher education programs. *The Journal of Environmental Education, 32*(1), 4–11. https://doi.org/10.1080/00958960009598666

McKeown, R., & Hopkins, C. (2002). Weaving sustainability into preservice teacher education programs. In W. F. Filho (Ed.), *Teaching sustainability at universities: Towards curriculum greening* (pp. 251–274). Peter Lang.

McMahon, P. (2013). *Feeding frenzy: The new politics of food*. Profile Book.

Mead, E., Gittelsohn, J., Kratmann, M., Roache, C., & Sharma, S. (2010). Impact of the changing food environment practices of an Inuit population in Artic Canada. *Journal of Human Nutrition and Dietetics, 23*(1), 18–26. http://doi.org/10.1111/j.1365-277X.2010.01102.x

Melaville, A., Berg, A. C., & Blank, M. J. (2006). *Community-based learning: Engaging students for success and citizenship*. Partnerships/Community. https://digitalcommons.unomaha.edu/slcepartnerships/40

Menzel, P., & D'Aluisio, F. (2007). *Hungry planet: What the world eats*. Material World.

Merriam, S. B. (2009). *Qualitative research: A guide to design and implementation*. Jossey-Bass.

Meyer, M. A. (2013). Hoea Ea: Land education and food sovereignty in Hawaii. *Environmental Education Research, 20*(1), 98–101. http://doi.org/10.1080/13504622.2013.852656

Mills, R., & Tomas, L. (2013). Integrating education for sustainability in pre-service teacher education: A case study from a regional Australian University. *Australian Journal of Environmental Education, 29*(2). 152–164. http://doi.org/10.1017/aee.2014.3

Miller, G. (2012). *Losing our touch: Annual report 2011/2012, part 2*. Environmental Commissioner of Ontario (ECO). http://docs.assets.eco.on.ca/reports/environmental-protection/2011-2012/2011-12-AR.2.pdf

Misselhorn, A., Aggarwal, P., Erickson, P., Gregory. P., Horn-Phathanothai, L., Ingram, J., & Wiebe, K. (2012). A vision for attaining food security. *Current Opinion in Environmental Sustainability, 4*, 7–17. https://doi.org/10.1016/j.cosust.2012.01.008

Mohtar, R. H. (2016, April). *The role of soils in global water and food security* [Policy Brief-16/11]. OCP Policy Center. https://www.policycenter.ma/sites/default/files/OCPPC-PB1611.pdf

Morgan, K., & Sonnino, R. (2013). *The School Food Revolution: Public food and the challenge of sustainable development*. Routledge.

Mount, P. (2012). Growing local food: Scale and local food systems governance. *Agriculture and Human Values, 29*, 107–121. http://doi.org/10.1007/s/10460-011-9331-0

Mueller, M. P. (2009). Educational reflections on the "Ecological Crisis": EcoJustice, environmentalism, and sustainability. *Science & Education, 18*, 1031–1056. http://doi.org/10.1007/s11191-008-9179-x

Murray, N. (2019, May 21). Food insecurity rising in Nunavut since launch of Nutrition North: Study. *CBC News*. https://www.cbc.ca/news/canada/north/food-insecurity-nunavut-nutrition-north-1.5140132

Nelson, A. (2010). Environmental education and ecology in a life science course for pre-service K-8 teachers using project wildlife in learning design. *The American Biology Teacher, 72*(3), 156–160. http://doi.org/10.1525/abt.2010.72.3.6

Nielson, W., Anderson, P., Hurley, A., Sabljack, V., Petereit, A. L., Hoskin, V., & Hoban, G. (2012). Preparing action competent environmental educators: How hard could it be? *Australian Journal of Environmental Education, 28*(2), 92–107. http://doi.org/ 10.1017/aee.2013.3

Nolet, V. (2013). Teacher education and ESD in the United States: The vision, challenges, and implementation. In R. McKeown, & V. Nolet (Eds.), *Schooling for sustainable development in Canada and the United States* (pp. 53–67). Springer.

Nunavut Bureau of Statistics. (2015). *2015 Nunavut Food Price Survey, Comparison of Nunavut & Canada CPI food price basket items (StatsUpdate)*. http://www.stats.gov.nu.ca/Publications/Historical/Prices/Food%20Price%20Survey%20StatsUpdate,%202015.pdf

O'Gorman, L., & Davis, J., (2013). Ecological footprinting: Its potential as a tool for change in preservice teacher education. *Environmental Education Research, 19*(6), 779–791. https://doi.org/10.1080/13504622.2012.749979

Ontario Ministry of Education. (1999). *Native Studies, grades 9 and 10*. http://www.edu.gov.on.ca/eng/curriculum/secondary/nativestudies910curr.pdf

Ontario Ministry of Education. (2000). *Native Studies, grades 11 and 12*. http://www.edu.gov.on.ca/eng/curriculum/secondary/nativestudies1112.pdf

Ontario Ministry of Education. (2002). *Interdisciplinary studies*. http://www/edu.gov.on.ca/eng/curriculum/secondary/interdisplinary1112.pdf

Ontario Ministry of Education. (2007a). *Ready set green! Tips, techniques, and resources from Ontario educators*. http://www.edu.gov.on.ca/eng/document/policy/readySetGreen.pdf

Ontario Ministry of Education. (2007b). *Shaping our schools shaping our future: Environmental education in Ontario Schools*. http://www.edu.gov.on.ca/curriculumcouncil/shapingschools.pdf

Ontario Ministry of Education. (2007c). *The Ontario curriculum grades 1-8: Science and technology*. http://www.edu.gov.on.ca/eng/curriculum/elementary/scientec18currb.pdf

Ontario Ministry of Education. (2008a). *The Ontario curriculum, grades 9 and 10: Science.* http://www.edu.gov.on.ca/eng/curriculum/secondary/science910_2008.pdf

Ontario Ministry of Education. (2008b). *The Ontario curriculum grades 11 and 12: Science.* http://www.edu.gov.on.ca/eng/curriculum/secondary/2009science11_12.pdf

Ontario Ministry of Education. (2008c). *Healthy food for healthy school's act.* http://www.edu.gov.on.ca/eng/healthyschools/lifestyle.html

Ontario Ministry of Education. (2009a). *The Ontario curriculum grades 9 and 10: Technological Education.* http://www.edu.gov.on.ca/eng/curriculum/secondary/teched910curr09.pdf

Ontario Ministry of Education. (2009b). *The Ontario curriculum grades 11 and 12: Technological education.* http://www.edu.gov.on.ca/eng/curriculum/secondary/2009teched112curr.pdf

Ontario Ministry of Education. (2009c). *Acting today, shaping tomorrow: A policy framework for environmental education in Ontario Schools.* http://www.edu.gov.on.ca/eng/teachers/enviroed/action.html

Ontario Ministry of Education. (2010a). *School food and beverage policy resource guide.* http://www.edu.gov.on.ca/eng/healthyschools/PPM150_Resource_Guide_2010.pdf

Ontario Ministry of Education. (2010b). *Policy /Program Memorandum No. 150.* http://www.edu.gov.on.ca/extra/eng/ppm/150.html

Ontario Ministry of Education. (2010c). *Green schools resource guide: A practical resource for planning and building green schools in Ontario.* http://edu.gov.on.ca/eng/policyfunding/GreenSchools_Guide.pdf

Ontario Ministry of Education. (2013a). *The Ontario curriculum, Social Studies, grades 1–6, History and Geography, grades 7–8.* http://www.edu.gov.on.ca/eng/curriculum/elementary/sshg18curr2013.pdf

Ontario Ministry of Education. (2013b). *The Ontario curriculum, Social Studies and Humanities, grades 9 to 12.* http://www.edu.gov.on.ca/eng/curriculum/secondary/ssciences9to122013.pdf

Ontario Ministry of Education. (2013c). *The Ontario curriculum, grades 9–10: Canadian and world studies: Geography, history and civics (Politics).* http://www.edu.gov.on.ca/eng/curriculum/secondary/canworld910curr2013.pdf

Ontario Ministry of Education. (2013d). *Supporting minds: An educator's guide to promoting students' mental health and well-being.* Draft version. http://www.edu.gov.on.ca/eng/document/reports/SupportingMinds.pdf

Ontario Ministry of Education. (2013e). *The K–12 school effectiveness framework (2013): A support for school improvement and student success.* http://www.edu.gov.on.ca/eng/literacynumeracy/SEF2013.pdf

Ontario Ministry of Education. (2015a). *The Ontario curriculum, grades 11 and 12: Canadian and world studies: Economics, geography, history, law and politics.* http://www/edu.gov.on.ca/eng/curriculum/secondary/2015cws11and12.pdf

Ontario Ministry of Education. (2015b). *The Ontario curriculum, grades 1–8: Health and Physical Education.* http://www.edu.gov.on.ca/eng/curriculum/elementary/health1to8.pdf

Ontario Ministry of Education. (2015c). *The Ontario curriculum, grades 9–12: Health and Physical Education.* http://www.edu.gov.on.ca/eng/curriculum/secondary/health9to12.pdf

Ontario Ministry of Education. (2017a). *Environmental Education: Scope and sequence of expectations, grades 1–8 and the Kindergarten program.* http://www.edu.gov.on.ca/eng/curriculum/elementary/environmental_ed_kto8_eng.pdf

Ontario Ministry of Education. (2017b). *Environmental Education: Scope and sequence of expectations, grades 9–12.* http://www.edu.gov.on.ca/eng/curriculum/secondary/environmental_ed_9to12_eng.pdf

Ontario Ministry of Education. (2019). *Frequently asked questions.* http://www.edu.gov.on.ca/eng/curriculum/secondary/commontwo.html#display

Ontario Ministry of Health and Long-term Care. (2011). *Open minds, healthy minds: Ontario's comprehensive mental health and additions strategy.* http://www.health.gov.on.ca/en/common/ministry/publications/reports/mental_health2011/mentalhealth_rep2011.pdf

Orr, D. (2011). *Hope is an imperative: The essential David Orr.* Island Press.

Oxford Online English Dictionary. (n.d). *Ecojustice.* Retrieved August 8, 2019, from https://www-oed-com.proxy.bib.uottawa.ca/view/Entry/59377?redirectedFrom=ecojustice#eid120737670

Pal, S., Haman, F., & Robidoux, M. A. (2013). The costs of local food procurement in two Northern Indigenous communities in Canada. *Food and Foodways, 12*, 132–152. http://doi.org/10.1080/07409710.2013.792193

Palmer, J. (1998). *Environmental Education in the 21st century: Theory, practice, progress and promise.* Routledge.

Papadimitriou, V. (1996). Environmental education within a science course in the initial education of primary teachers. *Environmental Education, 2*(1), 17–25. https://doi.org/10.1080/1350462960020102

Parfitt, J., Barthel, M., & Macnaughton, S. (2010). Food waste within food supply chains: Quantification and potential for change to 2050. *Philosophical Transactions of the Royal Society B, 365*, 3065–3081. http://doi.org/10.1098/rstb.2010.0126

Patel, R. (2008). *Stuffed and starved: The hidden battle for the World food system.* HarperCollins.

Pedretti, E., & Nazir, J. (2014). Tensions and opportunities: A baseline study of teachers' views of environmental education. *International Journal of Environmental and Science Education*, *9*(3), 265–283.

Pedretti, E., Nazir, J., Tan, M., Bellomo, K., & Ayyavoo, G. (2012). A baseline study of Ontario teachers' views of environmental and outdoor education. *Pathways: The Ontario Journal of Outdoor Education*, *24*(2), 4–12.

Pe'er, S., Yavetz, B., & Goldman, D. (2013). Environmental education for sustainability as values education. In M. Ben-Peretz, S. Kleeman, R. Reichenberg, & S. Shimoni (Ed.), *Embracing the social and the creative: New scenarios for teacher education* (pp. 135–153). Rowman & Littlefield.

Perikkou, A., Kokkinou, E., Panagiotakos, D. B., & Yannakoulia, M. (2015). Teachers' readiness to implement nutrition education programs: Beliefs, attitudes, and barriers. *Journal of Research in Childhood Education*, *29*, 202–211. http://doi.org/10.1080/02568543.2015.1009202

Peters, C. J., Bills, N. L., Wilkins, J. L., & Fick, G. W. (2008). Foodshed analysis and its relevance to sustainability. *Renewable Agriculture and Food Systems*, *24*(1), 1–7. http://doi.org/10.1017/S1742170508002433

Pimental, D., Hepperly, P., Hanson, J., Douds, D., & Seidel, R. (2005). Environmental, energetic, and economic comparisons of organic and conventional farming systems. *BioScience*, *55*(7), 574–582. https://doi.org/10.1641/0006-3568(2005)055[0573:EEAECO]2.0.CO;2

Pinstrup-Andersen, P. (2009). Food security: Definition and measurement. *Food Security*, (1), 5–7. https://doi.org/10.1007/s12571-008-0002-y

Pinstrup-Anderson, P., & Watson, D. D., II. (2011). *Food policy for developing countries: The role of government in global, national, and local food systems*. Cornell University Press.

Powers, A. L. (2004). Teacher preparation for environmental education: Faculty perspectives on the infusion of environmental education into pre-service methods courses. *The Journal of Environmental Education*, *35*(3), 3–11. https://doi.org/10.3200/JOEE.35.4.17-32

Powers, E. M. (2009). Combining social justice and sustainability for food security. In M. Koc, R. MacRae, L. J. A. Mougeot, & J. Welsh (Eds.), *For hunger-proof cities: Sustainable urban food systems* (pp. 30–37). International Development Research Centre.

Priyadharshini, E., & Carrington, V. (2016). Food, youth and education. *Cambridge Journal of Education*, *46*(2), 153-155. http://doi.org/10.1080/0305764X.2016.1161210

Ravindranath, M. J. (2007). Environmental Education in teacher education in India: Experiences and challenges in the United Nation's Decade of Education for Sustainable Development. *Journal of Education for Teaching, 33*(2), 191–206. https://doi.org/10.1080/02607470701259481

Reis, G., & Scott, J. (Eds.). (2018). *International perspectives on the theory and practice of environmental education: A reader.* Springer.

Reis, K., & Ferreira, J. (2015). Community and school gardens as spaces for learning social resilience. *Canadian Journal of Environmental Education, 20*, 63–77. https://cjee.lakeheadu.ca/article/view/1341/843

Rehber, E. (2012). Food for thought: "four Ss with one F": Security, safety, sovereignty, and shareability of food. *British Food Journal, 114*(3), 353–371. http://doi.org/ 10.1108/00070701211213465

Ricoveri, G. (2013). *Nature for sale: The commons versus commodities*. Palgrave Macmillian.

Robert, S. A., & M. Weaver-Hightower (Eds.). (2011). *School food politics: The complex ecology of hunger and feeding in schools around the world*. Peter Lang.

Robottom, I. (2013). Changing discourses in EE/ESD: A role for professional self-development. In R. Stevenson, M. Brody, J. Dillon, & A. E. J. Wals (Eds.), *International handbook of research on Environmental Education* (pp. 156–162). Routledge.

Rocha, C. (2008). *Brazil-Canada partnership: Building capacity in food security*. Center for Studies in Food Security, Ryerson University. https://www.ryerson.ca/foodsecurity/

Rose, N., & Lourival, I. (2019). Hegemony, counter-hegemony and food systems literacy: Transforming the global industrial food system. *Australian Journal of Environmental Education, 35* (2), 110–122. http://dx.doi.org/10.1017/aee.2019.9

Rosegrant, M. W., Koo, J., Cenacchi, N., Ringler,C., Robertson, R. Fisher, M., Cox, C., Garrett, K., Perez, N.D., & Sabbagh, P. (2014). *Food security in a world of natural resource scarcity: The role of agricultural technologies*. International Food Policy Research Institute, Washington, DC.

Rotz, S., & Kepkiewicz, L. W. (2018). Settler colonialism and the (im)possibilities of a national food policy. *Canadian Food Studies, 5*(3), 248–258. https://doi.org/10.15353/cfs-rcea.v5i3.275

Rutten, M. M. (2013). What economic theory tells us about the impacts of reducing food losses and/or waste: Implications for research, policy and practice. *Agriculture & Food Security, 2*(13), 1–13. https://doi.org/10.1186/2048-7010-2-13

Sagan, A. (2017, February 19). Food insecurity concerns grow in Canada as prices rise. *The Huffington Post*. http://www.huffingtonpost.ca/2016/02/19/low-income-families-struggle-to-feed-their-kids-healhty-foods-as-prices-rise_n_9271244.html

Sage, C. (2012). *Environment and Food*. Routledge.
Sage, C. (2013). The interconnected challenges for food security from a food regimes perspective: Energy, climate and malconsumption. *Journal of Rural Studies, 29*, 71–80. http://doi.org/10.1016/j.jrurstud.2012.02.005
Savin-Baden, M., & Howell Major, C. (2013). *Qualitative research: The essential guide to theory and practice*. Routledge.
Sauvé, L. (2002). Environmental education: Possibilities and constraints. *Connect, 27*(1/2), 1–4. https://pdfs.semanticscholar.org/43c1/c66b2f7427fd9b9ee826668f447026bc40e9.pdf
Schanbacher, W. D. (2010). *The politics of food: The global conflict between food security and food sovereignty*. Praeger.
Schiro, M. S. (2008). *Curriculum theory: Conflicting visions and enduring concerns*. SAGE.
Schurman, R., & Munro, W. A. (2010). *Fighting for the future of food: Activists versus agribusiness in the struggle over biotechnology*. University of Minnesota Press.
Shafiee-Jood, M., & Cai, X. (2016). Reducing food loss and waste to enhance food security and environmental sustainability. *Environmental Science & Technology, 50*, 8432–8443. http://doi.org/10.1021/acs.est.6b01993
Shallcross, T., Loubser, C., Le Roux, C., O'Donoghue, R., & Lupele, J. (2006). Promoting sustainable development through whole school approaches: an international, intercultural teacher education research and development project. *Journal of Education for Teaching, 32*(3), 283–301. http://doi.org/10.1080/02607470600782427
Shiva, V. (1993). *Monocultures of the mind: Perspectives on biodiversity and biotechnology*. Zed Books.
Shiva, V. (2005). *Earth Democracy: Justice, sustainability, and peace*. South End Press.
Shiva, V. (2013). *Making peace with the Earth*. Fernwood.
Smith, G. A. & Sobel, D. (2010). *Place and community-based education in schools*. Routledge.
Smoyer-Tomic, K. E., Spence, J. C., & Amrhein, C. (2006). Food deserts in the Prairies? Supermarkets accessibility and neighbourhood need in Edmonton, Canada. *The Professional Geographer, 58*(3), 307–326. https://doi.org/10.1111/j.1467-9272.2006.00570.x
Sobel, D. (2004). *Place-based education: Connecting classrooms and communities*. Orion Society.
Sonnino, R., Moragues Faus, A., & Maggio, A. (2014). Sustainable food security: An emerging research and policy agenda. *International Journal of Sociology of Agriculture and Food, 21*(1), 173–188. https://core.ac.uk/download/pdf/42512785.pdf

Sottile, F., Fiorito, D., Tecco, N., Girgenti, V., & Peano, C. (2016). An interpretive framework for assessing and monitoring the sustainability of school gardens. *Sustainability, 8*(801), 1–15. http://doi.org/10.3390/su8080801

Stake, R. E. (2009). The case study method in social inquiry: Chapter 1. In R. Gomm, M. Hammersley, & P. Foster (Eds.), *Case study method: Key Issues, Key Texts* (pp. 18–26). SAGE. https://dx-doi-org.proxy.bib.uottawa.ca/10.4135/9780857024367

Stanley, D., & Young, K. (2011). Conceptualizing complexities of curriculum: Developing a lexicon for Ecojustice and the transdisciplinarity of bodies. *Journal of Curriculum Theorizing, 27*(1), 36–47. https://journal.jctonline.org/index.php/jct/article/view/306/97

Stapleton, S. R. (2019). *Parent activists versus the corporation: A fight for school food sovereignty*. Agriculture and Human Values. https://bacademics.org/wp-content/uploads/2023/10/s10460-019-09955-w.pdf

Stapleton, S. R., & Cole, P. (2018). School lunch and student food insecurity: A teacher's observations and reflections. In S. Rice & A. Rud (Eds.), *Educational dimensions of school lunch* (pp. 157–171). Palgrave Macmillan.

Statistics Canada. (2020). *Food insecurity during the COVID-19 pandemic, May 2020* (Catalogue no. 45280001). Government of Canada. https://www150.statcan.gc.ca/n1/en/pub/45-28-0001/2020001/article/00039-eng.pdf?st=7iiEwmYj

Statistics Canada. 2022. (table). *Census Profile*. 2021 Census. Statistics Canada Catalogue no. 98-316-X2021001. Ottawa. Released February 9, 2022. https://www12.statcan.gc.ca/census-recensement/2021/dp-pd/prof/index.cfm?Lang=E (accessed February 22, 2022)

Steele, F. (2010). *Mainstreaming education for sustainability in pre-service teacher education in Australia: Enablers and constraints*. Australian Research Institute in Education for Sustainability (ARIES) for the Australian Government Department of the Environment, Water, Heritage, and The Arts (DEWHA). Canberra, Australia: DEWHA. http://www/aries.mq.edu.au/projects/preservice3/Pre-Service_Teacher_Ed3.pdf

Stevenson, R. B., Brody, M., Dillon, J., & Wals, A. E. J. (Eds.). (2013). *International Handbook of Research on Environmental Education*. Routledge.

Strand, K., Marullo, S., Cutforth, N., Stoecker, R., & Donohue, P. (2003). *Community-based research and higher education*. Jossey-Bass.

Swan, E., & Flowers, R. (2015). Clearing up the table: Food pedagogies and environmental education—Contributions, challenges and future agendas. *Australian Journal of Environmental Education, 31*(1), 146–164.

Swayze, N., Creech, H., Buckler, C., & Alfaro, J. (2012). *Education for sustainable development in Canadian faculties of education*. Council of Ministers of Education, Canada. https://www.iisd.org/pdf/2013/esd_canadian_faculties.pdf

Tarasuk, V., Li, T., & Fafard St-Germain, A.A. (2022). Household food insecurity in Canada, 2021. Toronto: Research to identify policy options to reduce food insecurity (PROOF). https://proof.utoronto.ca/

Tesh, S. N. (1988). *Hidden arguments: Political ideology and disease prevention policy*. Rutgers University Press.

Thaker, J., & Dutta, M. (2016). Millet in our own voices: A culturally-centred articulation of alternative development by DDS women farmers' sanghams. In S. Venkateswar & S. Bandyopadhyay (Eds.), *Globalisation and the challenges of development in contemporary India* (pp. 131–144). Dynamics of Asian Development. http://doi.org/10.1007/978-981-10-0454-4_7

The Economist Intelligence Unit. (2014). *Global food security index report 2014: Food loss and its intersection with food security*. https://www.google.com/search?client=safari&rls=en&q=The+Economist+Intelligence+Unit+(2014).+Global+food+security+index+report+2014:+Food+loss+and++++its+intersection+with+food+security.&ie=UTF-8&oe=UTF-8

Thomas, M. M. C., Miller, D. P., & Morrisey, T. W. (2019). Food insecurity and child health. *Pediatrics, 144*(4), 1–9. https://doi.org/10.1542/peds.2019-0397

Tilbury, D. (1995). Environmental education for sustainability: Defining the new focus of environmental education in the 1990s. *Environmental Education Research, 1*(2), 195–212. http://doi.org//10.1080/1350462950010206

Tilbury, D. (2004). Environmental Education for sustainability: A force for change in higher education. In P. B. Corcoran & A.E. J. Wals (Eds.), *Higher education and the challenge of sustainability: Problematics, promise and practice* (pp. 97–112). Kluwer Academic.

Tourangeau, W. (2017). GMO doublespeak: An analysis of power and discourse in Canadian debates over agricultural technology. *Canadian Food Studies/La Revue Canadienne des études sur alimentation, 4*(1), 108–138. http://doi.org/10.15353/cfs-rcea.v4i1.208

Trading Economics (2022). *Canada-Urban Population (% of total)*. https://tradingeconomics.com/canada/urban-population-percent-of-total-wb-data.html

Trexler, C. J., Johnson, T., & Heinze, K., (2000). Elementary and middle school teacher ideas about the agri-food system and their evaluation of agri-system stakeholders 'suggestion for education. *Journal of Agricultural Education, 41*(1), 30–38. http://citeseerx.ist.psu.edu/viewdoc/download?doi=10.1.1.487.4963&rep=rep1&type=pdf

Turner, R. J. (2015). *Teaching for EcoJustice: Curriculum and lessons for secondary and college classrooms*. Routledge.

United Nations, Department of Economic & Social Affairs, Population Division. (1978, October 14-26). *International Conference on Environmental Education: Tbilisi (USSR)*. Final Report. Paris. https://unesdoc.unesco.org/ark:/48223/pf0000032763

Unusan, N. (2007). Effects of a food and nutrition course on the self-reported knowledge and behaviour of preschool teacher candidates. *Early Childhood Education Journal, 34*(5), 323–327. http://doi.org/10.1007/s10643-006-0116-9

Vahabi, M., & Damba, C. (2013). Perceived barrier in accessing food among recent Latin American immigrants in Toronto. *International Journal for Equity in Health, 12*(1), 1–11. http://doi.org/10.1186/1475-9276-12-1

Van Petegem, P. V., Blieck, A., Imbrecht, I., & Van Hout, T. (2005). Implementing environmental education in pre-service teacher training. *Environmental Education Research, 11*(2), 161–171. https://doi.org/10.1080/1350462042000338333

Van Petegem, P. V., Blieck, A., & Boeve-De Pauw, J. (2007). Evaluating the implementation process of environmental education in pre-service teacher education: Two case studies. *The Journal of Environmental Education, 38*(2), 47–54. http://doi.org/ https://doi.org/10.3200/JOEE.38.1.47-54

Van Petegem, P. V., Blieck, A., & Van Ongevalle, J. V. (2007). Conceptions and awareness concerning environmental education: A Zimbabwean case study in three secondary teacher education colleges. *Environmental Education Research, 13*(3), 287–306. https://doi.org/10.1080/13504620701430331

Varga, A., Fu˝z Ko´szo, M., Mayer, M., & Sleur, W. (2007). Developing teacher competences for education for sustainable development through reflection: The environment and school initiatives approach. *Journal of Education for Teaching, 33*(2), 241–256. https://doi.org/10.1080/02607470701259564

Vivero-Pol, J. L. (2014). *The Food Commons Transition: Collective actions for food and nutrition security*. http://www.thebrokeronline.eu/Articles/The-food-commons-transition

Vogt, K. A., Patel-Weynand, T., Shelton, M., Vogt, D .J., Gordon, J. C., Mukumoto, C. T., Suntana, A. S., & Roads, P. A. (2010). *Sustainability unpacked: Food, energy, & water for resilient environments and societies.* Earthscan.

Wals, A. E. J. (2009). *United Nations Decade of Education for Sustainable Development (DESD, 2005-2014) review of contexts and structures for education for sustainable development: Learning for a sustainable world.* UNESCO.

Wals, A. E. J., & Kieft, G. (2010). Education for sustainable development: Research overview. *Sida Review, 13*, 1–54. https://www.sida.se/contentassets/c4e841051a02400baba535d878a82389/14994.pdf

Walker, S. (2014). Why Canada may be heading into a food security crisis. *Toronto Star.* https://www.thestar.com/news/insight/2014/10/12/canada_may_be_heading_into_a_food_security_crisis.html

Watts, J. (2019, February 21). World's food supply under' severe threat' from loss of biodiversity. *The Guardian.* http://www.theguardian.com/global-devlopemnt/2019/feb/21/worlds-food-supply-under-severe-threat-from-loss-of-biodiversity

Weaver-Hightower, M. B. (2011). Why education researchers should take school food seriously. *Educational Research, 40*(1), 15–21. http://doi.org/10.3102/0013189X10397043

Welch, R., McMahon, S., & Wright, J. (2012). The medicalization of food pedagogies in primary schools and popular culture: A case for awakening subjugated knowledges. *Discourses: Studies in the Cultural politics of Education, 33*(5), 713–728. http://doi.org/10.1080/01596306.2010.696501

Westfield, R. (2013, January 11). Half of world's food wasted, reports finds: Global effort needed to end harmful trend. *Toronto Star*, A1.

Williams, D. R. & Brown, J. D. (2012). *Learning gardens and sustainability education: Bringing life to schools and schools to life.* Routledge.

Wilson, S. (2012). Drivers and blockers: Embedding education for sustainability (EfS) in primary teacher education. *Australian Journal of Environmental Education, 28*(1), 42–56. http://doi.org/10.1017/aee.2012.5

Wittman, H., Desmarais, A. A., & Wiebe, N. (2011). *Food sovereignty in Canada: Creating just and sustainable food systems.* Fernwood.

World Food Summit. (1996). *Food security.* http://www.fao.org/filadmin/templates/faoitaly/docuemnts/pdf/pdf_food_security_concept_note.pdf.

Yavetz, B., D. Goldman, & Pe'er, S. (2009). Environmental literacy of pre-service teachers in Israel: A comparison between students at the onset and of their studies. *Environmental Education Research, 15*(4), 393–415.

Young, K. & Stanley, D. (2018). Integration, inquiry, and interpretation: A learning garden alternative placement and eco-mentorship program for pre-service teachers. In G. Reis & J. Scott (Eds.), *International perspectives on the theory and practice of Environmental Education: A reader.* (pp. 47–55). http://doi.org/10.1007/978-3-319-67732

ABOUT THE AUTHOR

Alishia A. Valeri has taught in both elementary and higher education classrooms in Canada and the United States. Her research areas are in Environmental Education, curriculum and food studies. She holds a PhD in Education from the University of Ottawa, Canada as well as a MA in Curriculum and Instruction from Saint Louis University and an Elementary Teaching Certificate from D'Youville College in the United States.

Printed in the USA
CPSIA information can be obtained
at www.ICGtesting.com
CBHW071926301124
18104CB00002BB/15